A HISTORY OF SOMERSET

Nunney Castle

THE DARWEN COUNTY HISTORY SERIES

A History of Somerset

ROBERT DUNNING

Drawings by Carolyn Lockwood

Cartography by Roy Cooney

PHILLIMORE

1983

Published by
PHILLIMORE & CO. LTD.
Shopwyke Hall, Chichester, Sussex

ISBN 0 85033 461 6

Printed in Great Britain by
BIDDLES LTD
Guildford, Surrey

and bound by
THE NEWDIGATE PRESS LTD
Dorking, Surrey

Contents

	List of Plates	..	..	..	..	..	..	..	..	7
	List of Maps	..	..	..	..	..	..	..	..	8
	Preface	..	..	..	..	..	..	..	..	9
	Introduction	..	..	..	..	..	..	..	..	11
I	Hunters to Heroes	..	..	..	..	..	..	..	15
II	The Age of Kings and Saints	..	..	..	..	..	21
III	The King and his People	..	..	..	..	..	..	29
IV	Exploiting the Land	..	..	..	..	..	..	..	35
V	Towns and Townsmen	..	..	..	..	..	..	43
VI	The Faith of the Flock	..	..	..	..	..	..	49
VII	Old Worlds and New	..	..	..	..	..	..	57
VIII	The Civil War	..	..	..	..	..	..	..	65
IX	Monmouth's Rebellion	..	..	..	..	..	..	71
X	And so to Bath	..	..	..	..	..	..	..	77
XI	Land, Labour and Learning	..	..	..	..	..	87
XII	The Twentieth Century	..	..	..	..	..	..	101
	Appendix One	..	..	..	..	..	..	..	107
	Appendix Two	..	..	..	..	..	..	..	108
	Appendix Three	..	..	..	..	..	..	..	109
	Appendix Four	..	..	..	..	..	..	..	117
	Sources for Further Study	..	..	..	..	..	..	118
	Index	..	..	..	..	..	..	..	..	122

Levels landscape

List of Plates

1. The Eclipse Track, Shapwick .. .. *facing page* 16
2. Stanton Drew, aerial view 16
3. Glastonbury Lake Village, iron age bowl .. *between pages* 16/17
4. Glastonbury Lake Village, iron age dice and shaker .. 16/17
5. The Somerset Levels 16/17
6. Cheddar Gorge, aerial view 16/17
7. Brean Down, aerial view 16/17
8. South Cadbury, aerial view .. .. *facing page* 17
9. Dolebury Warren, aerial view 32
10. Abbey Barn, Glastonbury .. .. .. *between pages* 32/33
11. Priddy Hurdles 32/33
12. Portrait of St Dunstan 32/33
13. Initial from Bishop Stillington's Register 32/33
14. Taunton Castle .. .. *facing page* 33
15. Farleigh Hungerford Castle 33
16. The Alfred Jewel (colour) 48
17. Head of Minerva (colour) 48
18. Dunster Dovecot .. .. *between pages* 48/49
19. Kingsbury Episcopi lock-up 48/49
20. Chew Magna church house 48/49
21. Congresbury Cross 48/49
22. Wells, aerial view 48/49
23. Glastonbury, aerial view 48/49
24. Montacute House (colour) .. .. *facing page* 49
25. Clevedon Court (colour) 49
26. Timberscombe church screen 64
27. Trull pulpit 64
28. *George* inn, Norton St Philip .. .. .. *between pages* 64/65
29. *George* hotel, Yeovil 64/65
30. Montacute Priory gatehouse 64/65
31. Kilve manor house 64/65

32. Sir Edward Rogers (colour) .. .. *facing page* 65
33. Thomas Lyte (colour) 65
34. Duke of Monmouth (colour) 65
35. Chilton Polden church 80
36. Ditcheat church 80
37. Tarr Steps .. .. *between pages* 80/81
38. Peat cutting 80/81
39. Claverton Manor 80/81
40. Tintinhull House 80/81
41. Watchet Harbour print .. .. *facing page* 81
42. Brympton D'Evercy, bird's eye view 81
43. Lord Portman 96
44. Henry Tuson 96
45. Railway near Bath .. .. *between pages* 96/97
46. Steam rollers 96/97
47. Somerset County Cricket Ground, Taunton 96/97
48. Bridgwater, carnival night 96/97
49. Bridgwater tile makers .. .. *facing page* 97
50. Oliver Stone, basket maker 97
51. John Leach, potter 97

The aerial photographs are reproduced by permission of John White, FBIPP, FRPS, West Air Photography, 23 Cecil Road, Weston-super-Mare. These plates are part of a 150,000 negative and transparency photographic library, mainly of South-West England and South Wales.

List of Maps

1. Physical features 12
2. Archaeological sites 14
3. Saxon towns and medieval urban growth 25
4. Medieval castles and fortified houses 37
5. Somerset religious houses, hospitals and colleges, *c.*1400.. 48
6. The gentry in the mid-16th century 59
7. Somerset in the Civil War 67
8. Monmouth's progress, 1680 and the Routes to
   Sedgemoor, 1685 73
9. Principal roads and postal routes, 1720 83
10. Inland navigation 92
11. The railway system, *c.*1910 96
12. Local government boundaries, 1974 105

Preface

To write about people and events of the past is to depend heavily upon the work of many who as custodians and editors of records, as archaeologists and antiquarians, have preserved, interpreted and made them available. The riches of Somerset's history in print are evident from the reading list at the end of this book.

Thanks for much help in the present goes first to David Bromwich and Steve Minnitt, the first for being more than a model local history librarian, the second for keeping me on a proper archaeological track and for suggesting suitable illustrations from the collections of the Somerset County Museum. Martyn Brown and Christopher Kitching provided me with, respectively, information on emigration and on the cloth fairs at Norton St Philip. The list of sheriffs in Appendix Three is based on the work of Mrs. S. W. Rawlins, first published by the Somerset Archaeological Society, the names after 1966 being provided by Miss Sylvia Langford.

Douglas Allen, Peter Birch, Brian Murless, Geoff. Roberts and Derek Seward each gave invaluable help with the plates; and the quality of Roy Cooney's maps and Carolyn Lockwood's drawings must be evident to every reader. The coats of arms are taken from Mrs. Rawlins' list of the county's members of parliament, also published by the Somerset Archaeological Society.

Why is a wife nearly always mentioned last? Mine has been encumbered with books and papers from the beginning, has typed most of the manuscript, and has sympathised, encouraged and supported throughout. This is small thanks and not to be accepted, as they say, as the only intimation.

Floor tiles from Glastonbury abbey

Introduction

The ancient county of Somerset, some 70 miles from east to west and 50 from north to south, lies on the southern shore of the Bristol Channel. A rough semi-circle of hills, old hard sandstones and slates form the heights of Exmoor and the Brendons in the far west; younger greensands, gault clays and gravels of the Cretaceous rocks of the Blackdowns mark the boundary with Devon; then a great sweep of limestone, beginning with the ridge of golden Ham stone and Yeovil sands in the south and continuing in the abrupt hills of the south-east; then the foothills of Salisbury Plain in the east, and finally the southern reaches of the Cotswolds. These hills stand guard over a delectable land.

They guard a county of astonishing variety: within their arc are three roughly parallel ridges—the Quantocks rising, a sandstone bastion to the west, the Mendips forming a commanding scarp of carboniferous limestone, dipping north-east towards Bristol in pockets of marl, coal measures and sandstone. In between are the Poldens, insignificant in any other country, but rising noticeably because they lie in some of the lowest and flattest land in England, the Somerset Levels.

Cheddar Pink (Dianthus gratianopolitanus)

And between these ridges and across these flat lands flow rivers—the Parrett with its tributaries, the southern Yeo, the Tone and the Isle; the Cary, the Brue, the Axe and the northern Yeo—now often running in man-created courses. Eight thousand years ago their waters flowed into a basin some 90 feet or more below the present level. Within some 2,000 years this basin was flooded by a significant rise in the level of the sea, and fingers of salt water reached deep into the countryside. The sea brought with it mud and silt which hardened to blue-grey lias, and then receded slightly. In the mud left behind in the basin reeds and sedge began to grow, producing over generations a landscape first of muddy pools and meandering rivers with willow and alder, and later of ash, oak and elm; and then with an increase in rainfall an acid soil supporting only heath and moss, forming as season followed season a rising peat bog filling the central basin, protected from all but the highest tides by a band of estuarine mud. There, in the heart of the county, are preserved most of the earliest traces of Somerset folk.

*   *   *   *   *

In the peat of the Levels and the caves of Mendip are also to be found the earliest traces of the county's flora and fauna. Fossils, bones

11

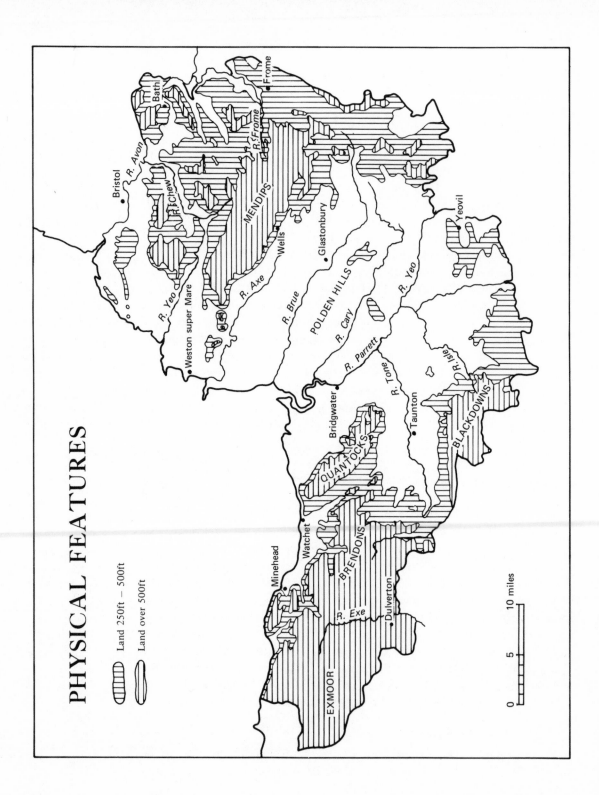

PHYSICAL FEATURES

Land 250ft – 500ft

Land over 500ft

Bath

Bristol

R. Avon

R. Chew

R. Yeo

Weston super Mare

R. Axe

Wells

R. Frome

Frome

MENDIPS

Glastonbury

R. Brue

POLDEN HILLS

R. Cary

R. Parrett

R. Yeo

Yeovil

R. Tone

Taunton

R. Isle

BLACKDOWNS

Bridgwater

QUANTOCKS

Watchet

Minehead

BRENDONS

R. Exe

Dulverton

EXMOOR

0   5   10 miles

and pollen reveal the earliest pattern of animal life and vegetation, a pattern whose development came to be closely related not only to changes in natural circumstances, but also to the relentless struggle of man to exploit the countryside, first for subsistence and then for profit. Climatic change and pollution are the main factors responsible for the disappearance of many plants which have grown in the country for thousands of years, making rare species such as the Somerset Hairgrass, the Cheddar Pink, or the Bath Asparagus, whose names are so clearly related to the county. Steepholm, less subject to human pressure than most places, has nevertheless almost lost the Wild Leek, which has grown there at least since the early 17th century (and which made the island's rabbits inedible), and the Peony, the latter nearly driven out by wind-sown sycamore. Industrial change now confines the Fuller's Teazel to small areas at Fivehead and Curry Rivel.

Unknown pressures in the past have undoubtedly deprived the county of animals common enough even in historic times: wolves, which may have given their name, for instance, to Woolminstone in Crewkerne, otters to the river Otter, and Otterford. Eighteenth-century parish accounts record payments of bounties to villagers in many parts of the county for the destruction of animals and birds considered pests, and large numbers of sparrows, hedgehogs and foxes were killed with evident enthusiasm. In the same accounts polecats and marten also appear and clearly did not survive the onslaught. And yet new plants, at any rate, take the place of old. Many species occupy temporary homes near docks, railways and mills, and do not survive for long, but the Giant Hogweed from south-east Asia has made itself at home in a few places, and the Pineapple Weed from North America is now almost a native, introduced with shipments of corn to Portishead at the turn of the century and spread rapidly from the 1920s onwards, sticking to motor tyres with the aid of West Country mud, and now to be found in farmyards, gateways and roadsides.

* * * * *

The natural history of the landscape is a less conventional part of the history of man in the countryside, and yet serves as an introduction to a more traditional story told through archaeological remains and written records. It is a story which begins with the earliest traces of human activity after the end of the Ice Age and continues as each day something is created and something is destroyed.

Bath Asparagus (Ornithogalum pyrenaicum)

ARCHAEOLOGICAL SITES

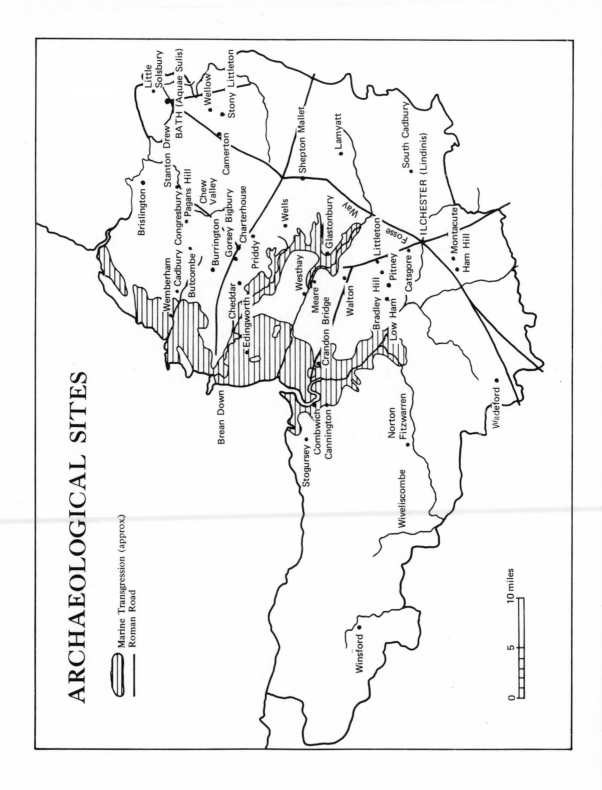

Marine Transgression (approx.)
Roman Road

0 5 10 miles

14

I Hunters to Heroes

The history of any county might properly begin with its formation as a shire, but people have lived in what later came to be Somerset perhaps for 240,000 years, and have left behind them hand axes as evidence of their craftsmanship and industry. Man, hunting reindeer, horse, bison and smaller animals and birds in the tundra of the high Mendips, the scrub of the lower slopes and the sedge of the valleys, used caves at Cheddar and Burrington for shelter, occupying some of them regularly and others but rarely, places to live and places to bury their dead.

After the end of the last Ice Age mixed oak forests covered much of the countryside except the exposed higher ground of the Mendips, Exmoor, and the Quantocks, where open woodland and scrub could survive. The rising sea level during the 7th millennium B.C. caused much of the Levels to be waterlogged, creating areas of reed fen in the valley floors, with salt marsh and extensive mudflats on the seaward end of the valleys. The hunter could have rich pickings in these differing environments. Deer, wild cattle, wild pig, and smaller game were to be found in the forests, with deer in summer browsing in the open hill country. The Levels were rich in wildfowl, notably swans and various kinds of duck, and fish such as trout, roach, pike, and perhaps salmon. Edible plants, berries and fruit could be found in the drier areas.

Bone 'calculator' from Gough's Cave, Cheddar

People moved around the countryside according to the seasons, summer probably being spent on the highest ground. In consequence camp sites were always temporary, often found today by the discovery of concentrations of small flint points and barbs of arrows, all that remain of the bows and arrows, wooden spears and traps which must have been their basic weapons. Flint knives and scrapers are also found, relics of the preparation of animal skins for clothing, and working in wood and bone. The flints themselves, coming from north Devon, south Somerset and Wiltshire, are evidence of the range of their trading contacts.

Flint arrowheads, flint and stone axes and pottery, capable of a wide variety of uses, and sometimes originating from as far afield as the Lake District and Cornwall, indicate the gradual development of a greater sophistication of life. Mendip has so far produced most traces of Neolithic man, and some of his pottery may well have been made in east Somerset and exported to Wiltshire. Flint scrapers suggest a number of sites, but few have been excavated. Those certainly identified

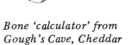

Neolithic flint axe, Sweet Track, Westhay

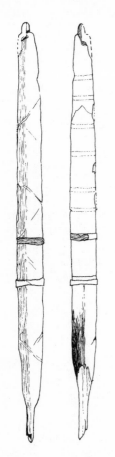

Part of Neolithic yew long bow, Meare Heath

include South Cadbury, the area now under the Chew Valley lake, a spot beside the springs at Wells, and several of the Mendip caves. Burials are more easily recognised, the chambered long barrows mostly in the north-east of the county, of which the best preserved is at Stoney Littleton. Two other remarkable features of Neolithic life are the stone circles at Stanton Drew, four 'henge' monuments known as the Priddy Circle, and a more modest 'henge' monument at Gorsey Bigbury, all presumably involving some kind of religious ritual.

The second feature, nothing short of a major engineering enterprise, showed that Neolithic man was a practical planner and craftsman, and Somerset can claim the densest concentration of his surviving work. Farmers, succeeding the ever-moving hunters and gatherers, settled on the slopes of the Poldens above the swampy Levels, cleared the land, reared cattle, sheep, goats and pigs, cultivated cereals and exploited the riches of the marshes. The exploitation was made possible by the construction of wooden trackways to cross the swamp. The earliest known track in Europe, if not in the world, is the Sweet Track, dating from *c.* 4000 B.C. which linked the Poldens with the island of Westhay. It was built of ash, oak and hazel poles, felled on the slopes with fire and stone axes, pegged in place with hazel, holly, alder, ash, and elm, and reinforced with blocks of peat and bunches of reed, together forming the base for a planked walkway. Tools and weapons found beside its route attest to its regular use, and its survival is due to the water which finally overwhelmed it.

The later trackways of the Levels changed with changing conditions. By 3600 B.C. the swamps had become shallower and birch and alder thickets dominated the scene. Hunters could move about between the shallow pools, needing much less substantial tracks. One hunter at this time left his weapon, the oldest English longbow yet discovered. Well before 3000 B.C., however, the landscape was again altered by increased flooding due to higher rainfall and by the development of the raised peat bog. Man's technology proved equal to the task, for he laid on the treacherous marsh a network of trackways, like the one found on Walton Heath, to provide a wide and strong passage for the movement of both men and cattle. Some of these trackways were built of hurdles, themselves the product of woodland management of coppiced hazel, and were made in exactly the same way as hurdles are made today.

Between 2000 B.C. and 650 B.C. the countryside was occupied by a people who used finer pottery than their predecessors, occupied river valleys, hill-top sites, and Mendip caves, and buried their dead in round barrows found in great numbers on the Mendips, the Quantocks, the Brendons and Exmoor. They continued to use flint and stone for their barbed and tanged arrowheads, daggers, scrapers, and axe hammers,

16

1. The Eclipse Track, Shapwick; built of wooden panels laid flat on the marsh surface about 1600 BC. (*Bryony Orme*)

2. Stanton Drew: a Neolithic ritual site of three stone circles, two avenues, a group of stones called the Grove and a fallen standing stone. (*West Air Photography*)

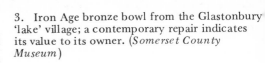
3. Iron Age bronze bowl from the Glastonbury 'lake' village; a contemporary repair indicates its value to its owner. (*Somerset County Museum*)

4. Iron Age bone dice and shaker from Glastonbury 'lake' village. The dice is not a cube and has only four faces numbered 3 to 6. (*Somerset County Museum*)

5. The Somerset Levels: Tadham moor near Wedmore. (*Douglas Allen Photography*)

6. Cheddar Gorge from the air; a spectacular fissure in the Mendip scarp. (*West Air Photography*)

7. Brean Down from the west, sheltering the mouth of the Axe and Uphill; Weston super Mare lies in the distance. (*West Air Photography*)

8   South Cadbury: Camelot from the air. The hillfort dominates the plain towards Ilchester.

perhaps importing polished axeheads from Wales, but they also introduced fine weapons and jewellery in bronze and occasionally in gold. Bronze axes, spearheads and daggers have been found beside ornamental torcs, bracelets and decorative pins. A hoard from Stogursey even contained scrap metal presumably on its way for re-casting. The hoard found at Norton Fitzwarren was within a defended enclosure which seems to have been an important focal point in the distribution of certain types of pottery and metal objects, and thus a place of some significance in the social and economic pattern of a wide area. Modern research, analysing the remains of the Bronze Age as never before, is suggesting the development of defined social strata, of farmers cultivating the river valleys, and of socially superior classes occupying and perhaps defending sites like Ham Hill and South Cadbury.

As bronze technology gave place to iron from *c.* 650 B.C., the picture of widespread farming, the exploitation of the Levels, and the re-occupation of the Mendip caves is broadened by the increase in hill-top settlement. Somerset's particular contribution to this development are the so-called 'lake villages' of Meare and Glastonbury, the open settlements of Pagans Hill and Butcombe, and the great hillforts of South Cadbury, Brean Down, Little Solsbury, and, in the west, probably Norton Fitzwarren.

The settlements of Meare and Glastonbury, at the marshy edges of the peat bog, were peopled by farmers who grazed cattle and sheep, went hunting, fowling and fishing, and were skilled in working natural materials, bronze, iron, and glass. They clearly enjoyed something better than a purely subsistence economy, for they left behind them amber, shale and glass beads, shale bracelets, and rings and brooches of bronze. The Roman invasion was not the abrupt arrival of an alien culture, but the culmination of a movement which had brought increasing sophistication to society. The hillforts probably formed foci in a regional sense, possibly acting as centres for trade and administration within a tribal framework, in which Somerset was divided between the territories of the Dumnonii in the west, the Durotriges in the centre and south, and the Dobunni in the north and east. By the time the Romans came in A.D. 43 the Dobunni seem to have abandoned hillforts in favour of sites on trade routes, but the Durotriges still defended Cadbury and Ham Hill, and their resistance to Roman domination was based on the old hillforts: the massacre at South Cadbury took place at the time of the revolt of Boudicca against Nero in eastern England in A.D. 60-61.

Gold torc, Hendford, Yeovil

In terms of chronology the rule of Rome was short, and scholars are now beginning to question how radical were the changes which Roman civilisation brought to the people of Somerset. Trade in Mendip lead

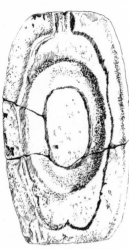

Stone mould for pewter dish, Camerton

had brought links with the Mediterranean world since the 1st century B.C. The Fosse Way, in contrast, was an innovation. It cut through the countryside by A.D. 49 with a chain of military forts probably at Bath, Camerton, Shepton Mallet, certainly at Ilchester, with outstations at Charterhouse on Mendip and at Wiveliscombe, and temporary garrisons at the old Durotrigian centres of South Cadbury and Ham Hill, either to demolish their defences or neutralise the threat they posed. Here was a statement of conquest.

The villa-farms so common in the rich valley of the Yeo around Ilchester also represent a new development, a new style of exploitation of the land, while the farming villages at Catsgore or Butcombe have more of the appearance of tradition. But the old ideas of villas as the homes of Gallic emigré landlords has been challenged. Enough is now known of both villas and farming hamlets and farmsteads like Butcombe to suggest the social organisation of their inhabitants. Hamlet and farmstead were the home of the kindred or extended family, like the Glastonbury 'lake village' of previous generations. Villas like those at Brislington, Littleton, Montacute, Pitney, Wadeford, and Wellow, and farmsteads like Bradley Hill suggest the continuation of a traditional joint proprietorship.

There was obvious continuity in farming, for the land and the climate were constants, the farms and villas around Ilchester producing cattle, with sheep on the higher ground around Somerton. The intensity of lead exploitation, the protection of the coastal plains from flooding and urban settlements were innovations. The amphitheatre at Charterhouse, the only one in the county, is enough to indicate the importance of Mendip lead to the Roman world; the Roman farms on the formerly flooded land at Edingworth, Wemberham, and in the Upper Axe valley point clearly enough to the skill with which Roman engineers grappled with large-scale projects throughout the Empire.

Ports at Combwich and Crandon Bridge, and centres of trade like Camerton are further evidence of Somerset as part of a wider world, but the great curative centre at Bath, with its temple of Sul-Minerva, and the temple sites at South Cadbury, Pagans Hill, Lamyatt, and Brean Down show that native religion continued under a Roman veneer. Bath now attracted visitors from distant parts of the Empire seeking relief from the healing properties of its waters. Roman Ilchester, Lindinis, on the other hand, seems to have been entirely new, planted at a strategic road junction in the rich plain of the Yeo and later serving as a regional capital for the Durotriges in a political and commercial sense.

Continuity is now the theme of much archaeological research. Urban Ilchester perhaps lasted until the late 5th century if the Byzantine

18

coins and pottery found there are sufficient indication, and its still unexplored cemetery may yet yield evidence of the earliest traces of Christianity in Somerset. Elsewhere there are signs of much earlier contraction, more easily explained in terms of population decline for reasons of plague and economic decline than the convenient withdrawal of Roman troops and the collapse of political systems. Archaeologists are looking to the revival of South Cadbury in the 5th and 6th centuries as a possible model for a return to a pre-Roman social and political pattern.

From the 16th century South Cadbury had other claims, and four centuries and more of tradition have established it as the Camelot of Arthurian Legend. Imported pottery from the eastern Mediterranean, North Africa, and southern France, and other signs of notable sophistication found at South Cadbury, Cadbury-Congresbury, and Glastonbury Tor in 5th- and 6th-century contexts, are seen by many as witness to the presence of Arthur, the *dux bellorum,* the greatest military hero the country had ever known. His last and greatest victory at Mount Badon, if not at Badbury Rings in Dorset, then at Bath and Little Solsbury, saved the Christian British of the south-west from the advancing pagan English and drove them back to occupy only a minor part of the country. Successor in the late 5th century to Ambrosius Aurelianus as military leader of the small British kingdoms which emerged from Roman Britain, Arthur is seen beyond the romantic legends of medieval England as a leader, even an emperor, whose exploits restored most of Britain to just Christian government. The rapid collapse of his 'empire' after his death could not detract from the memory of a golden age.

Somerset's place in the Arthur story is not entirely the product of a later age; the archaeological evidence from Glastonbury Tor fits with the tradition that it was the stronghold of Melwas, king of Somerset, who abducted Guinevere and kept Arthur at bay. The later claims of the monks of Glastonbury to possession of the mortal remains of Arthur and his queen are hardly compatible with the high romance of his passing, even if their commercial value was of the utmost significance in the rebuilding of the abbey. Geoffrey of Monmouth has Arthur, mortally wounded at Camlann, taken to the Isle of Avalon 'so that his wounds might be attended to'. Sir Thomas Malory has a different tale, of Bedivere carrying the dying king to a barge at the seaside, which carried him away. Tennyson, with Bedivere, saw

Cross from the 'grave' of Arthur

> the speck that bore the king
> Down that long water opening on the deep,
> Somewhere far off, pass on and on, and go
> From less to less and vanish into light.

*Caratacus stone,
Winsford Hill*

Surviving Celtic place-names and church dedications may indicate, as does the Arthur tradition, the survival of native Christian culture. As yet there are barely discernible signs of Christianity in Roman Somerset, with the possible exception of an inscription at Bath which could allude to a Temple-wrecking incident there by local christians in the 4th century. Christian burials in a previously pagan cemetery at Cannington, deliberately arranged around the body of a youth, is suggestive of more than a remote survival in the post-Roman period. So, too, is the Caratacus stone on Winsford Hill, its Latin inscription, CARATACI NEPUS, indicating both literacy and Christianity. The stone, dating perhaps to the 5th or 6th century, records one who in his generation was proud to recall that he was a descendant, in blood or in spirit, of that Caratacus who, fighting against the Roman invader, had been a hero among his people.

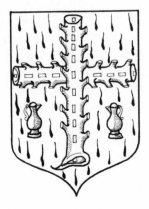

*'Arms' of St Joseph of
Arimathea*

II   The Age of Kings and Saints

When in the 12th century the monks of Glastonbury and Muchelney were trying to prove the antiquity of their houses they produced charters by which the early Saxon kings gave them parcels of their newly-conquered lands. These charters were not exactly forgeries, though the surviving texts are sometimes open to suspicion because dates or witnesses are incongruous. But if not exactly authentic and often copied inaccurately, they are clear declarations of historical truth. The two earliest charters of Glastonbury relating to Somerset recall how Cenwealh, king of the West Saxons (641-62), had granted to the monks the estate of Meare and the islands of Beckery, Godney, Marchey, and Nyland, probably in the last two years of his reign. That was 100 years after Cuthwine and Ceawlin, leaders of the advancing Saxons, had killed three British kings at the battle of Dyrham and captured three of their cities, including Bath; it was only eighty years after St Augustine began the conversion of the kingdom of Kent.

Part of Saxon cross shaft, Rowberrow church

The Saxons seem to have found their way westwards barred for a generation, but after the conversion of Cynegils at Dorchester (Oxon.) in 635 the church was firmly established among his people. Cenwealh, son of Cynegils, began the next advance west by defeating the British at Penselwood in 658, driving them as far as the Parrett. By 682 Saxon influence reached almost to Devon, for Glastonbury was given land in the front line, the island by the hill near the Tone whose British name *Cructan* was still remembered beside its new Saxon name *Crycbeorh*, now Creechbarrow, Taunton.

Witnesses to charters and the charters themselves show that an important part of the Saxon advance was the establishment of the church. The conquered lands west of Penselwood were at first part of the diocese of Winchester, whose bishop, Haedde (676–705), was witness to charters of King Ine to Glastonbury and Muchelney. On Haedde's death his huge see was divided and St Aldhelm, the renowned abbot of Malmesbury who had already founded a monastery at Frome *c.* 685, and who had almost certainly been preaching and teaching further west, was given episcopal oversight over the western end of the West Saxon kingdom with his seat at Sherborne. He remained both abbot and bishop until his death at Doulting in 709, whence the route taken by his body back to Malmesbury was marked every seven miles by a cross of stone.

St Aldhelm, Frome

When Aldhelm died, Ine (688–726) had been king for over twenty years. Conqueror of the British King Geraint in Cornwall in 710, Ine was founder of minsters or mission centres at Wells and Taunton, benefactor to Muchelney, and above all creator of the independence of Glastonbury and builder of the principal church there. His laws, almost the earliest English laws to survive, were drawn up with the advice and instruction of his father Cenred, of his bishops, Haedde of Winchester and Eorcenwald of London, of his ealdormen and chief councillors, and a great assembly of the servants of God. The laws reveal the formal social hierarchy of Saxon England, beginning with bishops, abbots, nobles, ealdormen, and officials set in authority over freemen, free peasants, household men, Welshmen, and slaves. The laws assume the existence of petty fighting and bands of marauders, strangers and foreigners wandering in the woods away from roads, escaping servants, traders in the countryside, and stolen and hidden meat. There are laws covering broken marrige contracts, the care of fatherless children and foundlings, and the recognition that a nobleman moving house would need to take with him his reeve, his smith, and his children's nurse.

Ine's successors in Wessex found themselves on occasions less secure, their power challenged by the Midland kingdom of Mercia and by the Britons in the far west. Aethelheard lost Somerton, perhaps his local capital, to the Mercians in 733, but defeated them in 740. His successor, Cynewulf (757–86) may have been forced to give Offa of Mercia land south of the Avon near the Mercian city of Bath, but for most of his long reign managed to remain respectably independent and spent his energies winning unnamed victories against the Britons. But a greater threat was on the horizon.

In 789 men from Norway landed in Dorset and killed a local official. For several years thereafter they attacked the north, leaving Egbert (802–39) to extend the influence of the West Saxons to the Humber. But large Danish raiding parties attacked Carhampton in 836 and 843, defeating the Saxons sent against them, though in 845 the ealdorman Eanwulf led the people of Somerset and their neighbours from Dorset to a victory at the mouth of the Parrett. Somerset people under their own ealdorman were there mentioned for the first time, and he led them until his death in 867 when he was buried in Glastonbury as befitted a man of his rank. Eanwulf's successor faced an even greater threat, for in the dreadful year 871 the Saxons were involved in nine pitched battles with the advancing Danes in Berkshire, Wiltshire, and Hampshire. Bishop Heahmund of Sherborne was among the fallen, and was buried at Keynsham; and his king, Ethelred, followed him to the grave.

22

To Ethelred succeeded his remarkable brother, Alfred, and the most dramatic event in his reign belongs peculiarly to Somerset. In 878 the Danes were in strength both in Wiltshire and Devon; Somerset was virtually isolated and many of her local leaders in flight, though the ealdorman Aethelnoth stayed with a small force, according to a local chronicler 'in a certain wood'. Alfred himself sought refuge in the 'woods and fen-fastnesses' of the Levels, and even there survived only with difficulty, 'for', wrote his biographer, Asser, 'he had nothing to live on except what he could seize by frequent raids, either secretly or openly, from the pagans and even from the Christians who had surrendered to the rule of the pagans'. The story of the abstracted king allowing the peasant woman's cakes to burn is suitable local colour. Yet from this extremity at Easter 878 Alfred with some local followers left his stronghold at Athelney, the island of the princes, and rode into Wiltshire to win a great victory at Edington. It was fitting that Guthrum, the Danish leader, and 30 others were baptised at the church on another island, at Aller, the church of the royal estate which covered the ridge from Somerton to Langport; fitting, too, that the new converts should be publicly recognised at a ceremony on the royal island of Wedmore attended by the Somerset ealdorman, and that the formal peace agreement made between Alfred and Guthrum should have been named after Wedmore, even though it was drawn up perhaps ten years after the English victory.

Statue of King Alfred, Winchester

The remarkable qualities of Alfred belong to the whole of England. His particular contributions to Somerset were the foundation, or perhaps the re-foundation, of the abbey on the fortified island of Athelney, and the Alfred Jewel, found nearby in 1693. Monastic life in Alfred's kingdom had for some time been virtually abandoned, perhaps because of the Danish raids, perhaps because of 'the nation's too great abundance of riches of every kind' (Bishop Asser was not certain which). Alfred therefore imported foreign monks for his new abbey—John the Old Saxon as the first abbot, and other monks from Gaul, including some children who were taught in a new school there, and even a young man 'of the pagan race'. The monastery survived until 1539, but no trace of it now remains above ground.

The Alfred Jewel still survives. Its exact purpose may never be proved, but it may perhaps have been the end of one of the aestels or pointers for public reading and study of an important book. An aestel, worth 50 mancuses (the price of 300 sheep or 50 oxen), accompanied each copy of the king's translation of Pope Gregory's *Pastoral Care,* sent to every diocese in his kingdom. The work was designed to play an important part in the revival of scholarship in the kingdom, for young men were to be encouraged to learn English, and those destined for the church to study Latin. The value of the pointer showed how important the king considered the book to have been.

The Peace of Wedmore was not the end of fighting, and fortifications at Bath, Axbridge, Lyng (at the end of a causeway leading to Athelney) and Watchet were part of a chain of strongholds providing some sort of defence against invasion. But in 914 despite these defences a Danish force from Brittany landed east of Watchet and also at Porlock. The raiders were beaten off with heavy losses, and the survivors had to swim for their boats, and then spent some time, according to the *Anglo-Saxon Chronicle,* on the island of Steepholm in the Bristol channel.

St Dunstan in stained glass, Cothelstone church

Somerset, where Alfred himself had owned estates along the threatened coast at Carhampton, Kilton, Cannington and Burnham, as well as at Wedmore and Crewkerne, continued to be an important part of the kingdom under his successors. Cheddar, with its religious community and royal palace complex, was the scene of at least three meetings of the *witan,* and Somerton of a fourth during the reigns of Edmund, Eadred (who died at Frome), Eadwig and Edgar, and it was at Bath, the ancient borough of Acemannesceaster, that Edgar 'with a great company, was consecrated king . . .'. The ceremony, probably devised by St Dunstan, has been the model for English coronations ever since. Edgar died two years later and was buried, like Edmund, at Glastonbury. His body was later removed to a copper and gilt tomb in the magnificent eastern chapel of the abbey church built by Abbot Bere and embellished by Abbot Whiting.

The link between the Saxon kings and Glastonbury, so evident from the gifts later showered upon the house, was never so close nor so significant for the history of the whole country as during the time of Dunstan. Dunstan was born at Baltonsborough, near Glastonbury, of royal stock in 909, the year when his relative, Athelm, was consecrated the first bishop of the Somerset people. He was introduced to the royal household under Athelstan about 925. About 943, after King Edmund's miraculous escape from death on the cliffs at Cheddar while hunting, Dunstan was appointed 'abbot' of the community at Glastonbury and there re-established the Benedictine Rule of monasticism which became the model for the religious life throughout England. The chosen counsellor of Eadred, under whom Glastonbury became the repository of the royal treasure and archives, he was banished by Eadwig, and spent his exile at Ghent, learning of the monastic revival on the Continent. He was recalled in 957 by Eadwig's brother, Edgar, then king of Mercia, and was appointed bishop first of Worcester (957–61), then of London (959–61). Edgar succeeded his brother as king of Wessex in 959, and in the following year Dunstan became archbishop of Canterbury.

24

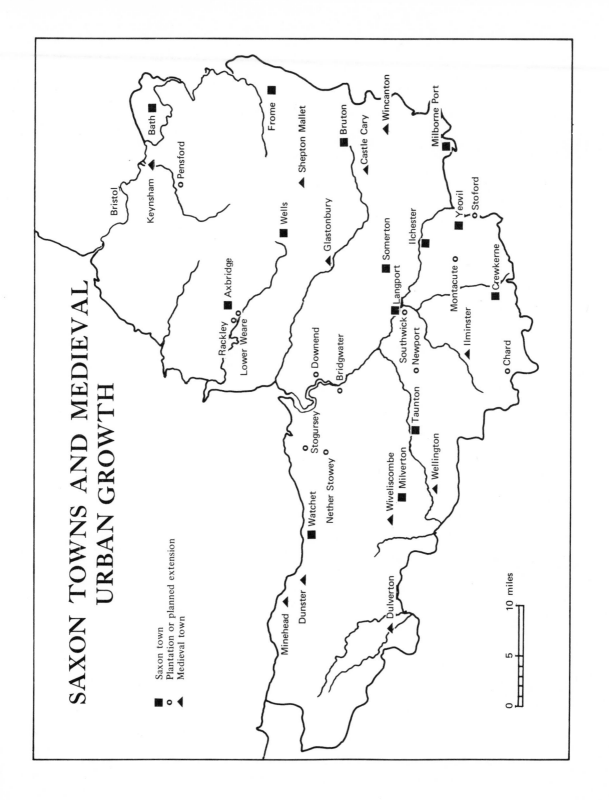

SAXON TOWNS AND MEDIEVAL URBAN GROWTH

■ Saxon town
○ Plantation or planned extension
▲ Medieval town

Bristol

Bath

Keynsham

Pensford

Frome

Shepton Mallet

Bruton

Castle Cary

Wincanton

Milborne Port

Wells

Glastonbury

Somerton

Ilchester

Yeovil
Stoford

Axbridge

Rackley
Lower Weare

Downend

Bridgwater

Langport
Southwick
Newport

Montacute

Crewkerne

Ilminster

Chard

Stogursey

Nether Stowey

Watchet

Wiveliscombe

Milverton

Taunton

Wellington

Minehead

Dunster

Dulverton

0   5   10 miles

25

Viking gilt copper-alloy disc brooch, Pitney

Dunstan, the great monastic leader, belongs to the history of the nation, like Alfred, and his talents as musician, illuminator, designer, and metal-worker were enjoyed not simply by Glastonbury. The consequences of his work there, however, may be shown in the fact that four of its monks became bishops of Wells in the 10th century, and of the six archbishops who succeeded him at Canterbury, five came from Glastonbury, and the sixth was one of Dunstan's relatives, St Alfheah, probably a native of Twerton, and former monk and abbot of Bath, who was martyred by the Danes at Greenwich in 1012.

By that time the threat of invasion had again become a reality. Attacks on the south coast had begun in 980, early in the long reign of Ethelred II (978–1016), and Dunstan 'after long and anxious thought' transferred the relics of St Aldhelm, 'reverently wrapped in scarlet and fine linen,' from their shrine to a plain tomb at Malmesbury, lest they proved too much of a temptation to plundering Danes. In 988, the year of his own death, Watchet was ravaged, and again in 997, when the Danish army 'did much damage there, burning and slaying'. By 1011 the army had overrun the kingdom as it had done under Alfred, Danish control reaching over much of Wiltshire. Small wonder that there is a particular concentration of mints in Somerset producing coin in Ethelred's reign, and that at least one was transferred from its vulnerable site at Ilchester to the refortified hilltop of South Cadbury, where coins were minted between *c.* 1009 and 1019. The purpose of this expanded production is clear, for many of those coins are still to be found in Scandinavia: they were the tribute extracted from a constantly defeated king.

Swein Forkbeard altered the struggle by his arrival in 1013 to claim the kingdom from Ethelred. He received the submission of the western shires at Bath, but died in the following year, leaving his son, Cnut, to continue his policy. Ethelred himself died early in 1016, but his son, Edmund Ironside, 'stoutly defended his Kingdom while his life lasted', fighting at Penselwood the first of six engagements. An agreement between Edmund and Cnut left Edmund ruling Wessex, but he died before the end of the same year, and was buried at Glastonbury. Somerset, like the rest of Wessex, was ruled by Cnut. The Cadbury moneyers struck coins for a while in the name of the new king, but soon transferred their work to the market centres of Bruton and Crewkerne.

Silver penny of Ethelred, struck by Winas at Cadbury

The orderly rule of Cnut (1016–1035) brought Wessex under Earl Godwine. He and his sons, Swein and Harold, established a large estate in Somerset. Their doubtful allegiance to Edward the Confessor brought banishment for all three in 1051, but Harold returned in 1052, defeating a royal force after landing at Porlock. Somerset followed

26

Earl Harold when he succeeded the Confessor as king in 1066. The fragment of the True Cross found on St Michael's Hill at Montacute became the object of Harold's particular interest, and its name was the war cry of the English troops at the battle of Hastings.

Montacute, perhaps not surprisingly, was one of the places where there was active opposition to that last great wave of conquest, and the count of Mortain's castle there was besieged in 1068. The Saxon sheriff, Tofig, and the Saxon military leader, Eadnoth the Staller, supported William the Conqueror when Harold's sons attempted to regain their father's kingdom. Eadnoth fell fighting for his new king, and the people of Somerset found themselves again at the mercy of outsiders.

Dragon of Wessex

The king himself took the lands like Somerton and Cheddar, Wedmore and Axbridge, Frome and Bruton, once held by the royal house of Wessex. He seized great estates like Dulverton, Old Cleeve, Congresbury, and Keynsham, which had belonged to Earl Harold, or his sister, Edith. Saxon landowners gave place to Norman bishops and Norman lords, their names declaring their origins across the Channel. Walter de Dowai, Roger de Courceulles, William de Mohun, William de Falaise, and the count of Mortain were among the great tenants-in-chief. The count, half-brother to King William, had a vast holding spreading across the south of the county, with its centre at Montacute. Among the men who came to England with him were Alfred the butler, and Robert the constable, Bretel de St Clair, and Drew de Montagud. Two by their names suggest their relationship with their lord, two their origins in the countryside of Normandy. But they came as permanent settlers in a new land, and left there, too, more than a memory of their existence. Bretel held, among other places, a manor called Ash, which he or others distinguished from other places of that name by the addition of his; thus was Ashbrittle born. Robert and Drew were the ancestors of the Beauchamps and the Montacutes, two families who belong to the very heart of medieval Somerset, two families still remembered at Hatch Beauchamp and Shepton Montague among the many Somerset place-names which owe their euphony to their Norman owners.

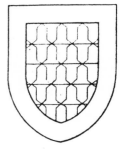

Arms of Beauchamp of Lillesdon

vii. TERRA EDWARDI SARISBER'.

EDWARD SARISBER' ten de rege HUNTONE. Vlueua teneb
T.R.E. 7 geldb p. x. hid. Tra. e. x. car. In dnio st. iij. car. 7 x.
serui. 7 xij. uilli 7 xx. bord cu. vi. car. Ibi. ij. molini redd
xxxiiij. sol. 7 xij. ac pa. Silua. i. leu lg. 7 dim leu lat.
In Bade. ij. dom. una redd. vij. den 7 obolu. Oli. x. lib. m ual. xij. lib.

Ipse. E. ten NORTONE. Luing teneb T.R.E. 7 geldb p. x. hid.
7 tra. e. x. car. In dnio st. iij. car. 7 iij. serui. 7 iij. uilli 7 xiij.
bord cu. iij. car. Ibi molin redd. v. solid. 7 xx. ac pa. 7 ualt
pasture. Silua. i. leu lg. 7 tantd lat. Oli. vi. lib. modo. vij. lib.
De his xx. hid ded rex. E. p dicto luing. ij. carue trg.

TERRA ERNVLFI DE HESDING.

ERNVLFVS de hesding ten de rege WESTONE. Edric teneb
T.R.E. 7 geldb p. v. hid. Tra. e. vij. car. In dnio st. ij. car. 7 x.
serui. 7 vi. uilli 7 i. bord cu. iij. car. Ibi molin redd. xx. solid.
7 xxij. ac pa. 7 lx. ac pasture. 7 xxx. de silue. In Bade. iij. dom
redd xx vij. den. Totu oli 7 modo ual. viij. lib. V

Engeler ten de brn TICHEHA. Edric teneb T.R.E. 7 geldb
p. i. hida 7 iij. virg. Tra e. iij. car. Ibi st. iij. uilli 7 i. bord
7 ij. seruus. 7 vi. ac pa. Silua. iij. qrz lg. 7 una qrz lat. Val xl. sot.

Ingelramn' ten de br. REDDENE. Edric teneb T.R.E. 7 geldt
p una hida. Tra. iij. car. q ibi st in dnio. 7 iiij. serui. 7 xx viij.
bord. Ibi. ij. molini redd. xv. solid. 7 xx. ac pa. 7 xxx. ac
pasture. Silua. i. leu lg. 7 tantd lat. Olim 7 m ual. iiij. lib.

TERRA GISLEBERTI FILII TVROLDI.

GISLEBERTVS filius Turoldi: ten de rege CHINESTOCH.
7 Osbn' de eo. Edric teneb T.R.E. 7 geldb p una hida 7 dim.
Tra. e. ij. car. q ibi st in dnio. 7 ij. serui. 7 ij. bord. 7 xx. ac pa.
7 x. ac silue minute. Olim. xx. sol. modo ual. xxx. solid.

Walter ten de. G. TUMBELI. Edric teneb T.R.E. 7 geldb
p. v. hid. Tra. e. v. car. In dnio. e. i. car. 7 ij. serui. 7 vi. uilli
7 iiij. bord 7 iiij. coscez cu. iij. car. Ibi molin redd. xxx. den.
7 xxx. v. ac pa. pastura. i. leu lg. 7 dim leu lat. 7 tantd silue
Q do recep. ualb. c. sol. modo tntd.

Ide ten' ESTONE. Edric teneb T.R.E. 7 geldb. p. i. hida. Tra. e. i.
car. q ibi. e. cu. iij. bord. Redd. xxx. solid.

III The King and his People

Like their Saxon predecessors, medieval kings were always on the move, travelling between royal manors, living at the expense of others, and ensuring, when so much depended on the king's personal qualities, that government was strong and effective. Somerset saw less of the Norman kings, for Wessex was no longer the heartland of the royal house, but Stephen was obliged to take action in the county in 1138 when, loyally supported by his brother, Henry, abbot of Glastonbury and bishop of Winchester, and by Robert of Lewes, bishop of Bath, he led troops against Ralph Lovel of Castle Cary, the 'predatory and utterly unreliable' William Mohun of Dunster, and the defenders of East Harptree castle. Bishop Robert's men captured the rebel, Geoffrey Talbot, but the bishop himself was taken by trickery, and barely escaped with his life.

King John, from his effigy in Worcester cathedral

King John knew well how the presence of the king was vital in bolstering royal authority, and he came to Somerset at least a dozen times. In the summer of 1205, for instance, he was at Sock Dennis on 28 August. He spent part of the next day at nearby Ilchester, and then moved on to Curry Mallet, and was at Taunton on the 31st. On the next two days he was in Bridgwater, and he moved from there to Glastonbury, Wells, East Harptree, and then on to Bristol. He went to Wells at least nine times, on the first occasion in 1201 hearing cases in the assize court. Where he stayed on his journeys can only be guessed —the castles at Taunton, Bridgwater, and Harptree, the abbey at Glastonbury, and perhaps at Wells in the house of one of his clerks, Hugh of Wells.

John's son, Henry III, spent the summer of 1250 in the West Country, coming from Sherborne to Montacute on 3 August, and moving to Ilchester and thence into Devon. He came back again on the 13th to Bridgwater, on the 15th and 16th to Glastonbury, to Wells on the 17th, and Chew Magna—perhaps to the bishop's manor house there—on the 18th. On another visit, in 1256 to Bath, he ordered one of his foreign knights, Fortunatus de Lucca, to be thrown into the baths, but afterwards he gave the man a mark to buy a new robe. During the same period King Henry's rule in other parts of the country was challenged by Simon de Montfort and other barons, but only a few men from Somerset were involved. Some few from west Somerset followed the rebel, Adam Gurdun, constable of Dunster; Peter de

Montfort and Humphrey de Bolesdun were killed at Evesham, fighting against the king; and Walter de Kent, bailiff of Taunton, Sir Ralph Bluet of Hinton Blewett, Thomas Beaufiz of Nynehead, and Brian de Gouvis of Kingsdon were all declared to be rebels.

Edward I and his queen spent Easter 1278 at Glastonbury, where Abbot John Taunton showed them the remains of Arthur and Guinevere, which were then solemnly placed in wooden chests by the high altar. In December 1285 Edward spent a few days at Queen Camel and Somerton, both estates belonging to the queen. Some of his most prominent ministers had Somerset connections: Robert Burnell was Chancellor of England from 1274 until 1292, and Bishop of Bath and Wells from 1275; he died at Berwick in 1292, where Edward was deciding between the rival claimants to the throne of Scotland. Burnell was followed in office by John de Langton, Treasurer of Wells, at whose house in Martock the Great Seal of England was kept in 1297 when he went abroad. Two later bishops of Bath and Wells also served Edward I, William of March as Treasurer of England (1290-95), and John Droxford as Keeper of the Wardrobe (1295-1309).

A royal visit in the long reign of Edward III brought the king and queen from Wareham to Glastonbury in December 1331, and three days later to Wells. There they spent Christmas and the New Year at the bishop's palace, Bishop Ralph of Shrewsbury having to move out to Wookey to make room for the royal household.

By the mid 14th century the king's rule and the king's justice were being administered through a complicated system of courts and officers, both central and local, which in 1381 had to withstand serious revolt in many parts of England. Only 14 Somerset people were apparently implicated, including Thomas Engilby, a hosier, a scrivener, a weaver, a sheathmaker, and a soothsayer. Engilby and his men went on the rampage in Bridgwater and Ilchester, attacking the Master of St John's hospital, Bridgwater, John Sydenham of Sydenham and James Audley, and destroying their estate records as their fellow revolutionaries attacked landlords in other parts of the country. They beheaded two men in Bridgwater and put their heads on spears on the town bridge.

There seems to have been some sympathy in the county for the Welsh rebels under Owen Glendower, and hundreds of sheep and cattle were somehow collected at Banwell, but were found by the sheriff before they were embarked at Clevedon. It was probably not very serious when Canon Richard Bruton publicly declared at Wells in 1415 that he supported the plot against the life of Henry V and was prepared to spend £6,000 to depose him. The story was put about by John Williams of Cardiff, but apparently no action was taken against him.

30

The breakdown of law and order under Henry VI was at least in part the consequence of the king's own personality. Effective government was impossible in the hands of a pious weakling who, when he visited Bath in 1449, was embarrassed by the mixed nude bathing insisted upon by enterprising locals. County rivalries fed on national politics. In 1451 the earl of Devon, supporting the duke of York's claim to power, left Taunton with a force of 5,000 men to attack the loyalist earl of Wiltshire in east Somerset and then return to lay siege to Taunton castle, defended by the Lancastrian Lord Bonville. Bonville surrendered to the duke of York after three days, but the rivalry continued, and bands of men supporting Devon and York appeared in 1452 at Yeovil, Ilminster, and Broadway.

Badge of Dean Gunthorpe, Old Deanery, Wells

A few years of Yorkist rule could not repair the damage to royal government, and Edward IV found himself challenged by Warwick the Kingmaker and his own brother (and possible replacement), George, duke of Clarence. As he pursued them from York he came to Wells on 11 April 1470, to find that the rebels had already left for Exeter and France. All, friend and foe, made offerings at the cathedral or at the dean's chapel, and the receiver, recording their generosity, was careful to describe both the king and his brother as 'illustrious', a sensible precaution in such uncertain times. Indeed, Clarence was back at Wells within a year, staying at the bishop's palace as he raised troops for the restored Henry VI.

Henry VII understood how important was the constant presence of an effective king. He was at Wells in 1491 with a retinue which included Archbishop Morton, and was there again in 1497 in the aftermath of the Warbeck rebellion. His stay at the newly-built deanery may have been an honour for Dean Gunthorpe, but the citizens of Wells had to produce over £313 in fines for their disloyalty in giving countenance to the rebel. One of the last royal visitors to Somerset in the medieval period must have been the young Catherine of Aragon, on her way from Plymouth to marry Prince Arthur in 1501. She stayed overnight in Crewkerne, probably in the home of Richard Surland, one of the town's three parsons, and sub-dean of the chapels royal. Surland's successor, Christopher Plummer, was later to be Catherine's chaplain, and spent some months in the Tower of London for taking her part in the great question of the king's divorce.

*   *   *   *   *

Government, at home and abroad, needed money, and the demands of medieval kings took cash from purses, corn from barns, and men from their homes. Taxation records are as useful to historians as they

31

Arms of Sir Peter Courtenay

were to the collectors, as lists of names of villagers, and the unpopular poll taxes are, where they survive, the best guide both to total population and to the rich and poorer quarters of our towns. Military service and the direction of labour obviously affected fewer people, but the exactions of the royal victuallers, searching not always scrupulously for supplies for troops, were hard to bear in a subsistence economy.

Edward I's campaign in West Wales in 1277 called only 11 knights and four sergeants from the county, but Bridgwater mariners were involved in taking food to the troops. A few men were summoned to Rhuddlan in 1282, and to Carmarthen in 1283, and Bridgwater and Dunster men were called for help to raise a fleet against France in 1295 and 1297. A scheme to raise one foot soldier from each township against the Scots in 1311 was probably abandoned, but Somerset and Dorset together had to supply 2,000 quarters of wheat for the campaign. Stephen le Blund was commissioned for a similar task in 1316, finding supplies for the men fighting the rebel, Llewellyn Bren, in Glamorgan. In 1322 the county was required to find as many as 2,000 men.

Unknown numbers fought for Edward III in France or defended their country at home, and ships from Somerset ports transported troops and provisions, engaged in piracy, and fought in more conventional engagements at sea. Sir Ralph of Middleney served under Somerset's most distinguished military leader, William de Montacute, earl of Salisbury, in France in 1338, and then returned to reveal bad habits in public life. John de Ralegh of Nettlecombe was pardoned in 1347 for 'departing from the army overseas' without permission. Much more respectable was Sir Peter Courtenay of East Coker, who was knighted by the Black Prince in Spain in 1366, but was captured by the Spanish and held to ransom when the fleet was destroyed in 1369. John de la Mare of Nunney is said to have built his castle there in the 1370s from the profits of war, and to have modelled it on the Bastille in Paris; and Sir Matthew Gournay, buried with great magnificence in the now vanished castle chapel at Stoke sub Hamdon, made his name and fortune by his sword. He it was who in 1393 agreed to employ Simon de Ralegh of Nettlecombe and an archer as part of the contingent he took under John of Gaunt to Guienne. A bond in £40 ensured that Matthew would be compensated should Simon behave like his father had done.

In the Agincourt campaign Henry V was ably served by Sir Hugh Luttrell of Dunster, Lieutenant of Harfleur, who had already served the Crown in Ireland, and against Owen Glendower in Wales. Sir Walter Hungerford of Farleigh Hungerford fought at Agincourt and was later admiral of the fleet. Sir Edward Hull of Enmore served Henry VI in

Effigy of Sir Hugh Luttrell, Dunster church

9. Dolebury Warren, Churchill: the Iron Age hillfort on its spectacular Mendip site, later mined and used as a rabbit warren. (*West Air Photography*)

10. The medieval barn, Glastonbury, one of several on the Glastonbury estates and now part of Somerset Rural Life Museum. (*Somerset County Council*)

11. The hurdles at Priddy *en fête*: the August sheep fair will cease for ever, they say, if the hurdles are not kept in readiness on the green. (*Michael Aston*)

12. St Dunstan at the feet of Christ: mid 10th-century drawing by the saint himself (from Bodleian MS Auct. F 432, f 1). (*Bodleian Library Oxford*)

13. The hunter and the hunted; the first initial drawn by a clerk in Bishop Stillington's register, 1466. (*Somerset Record Office*)

14. Taunton castle from the north-west: the *camera* of Bishop William Ralegh of Winchester 1246-9. (*Joseph Thomason*)

15. The Lady Tower, Farleigh Hungerford castle, built by Sir Thomas Hungerford by 1383. The tower may have held the captive Lady Elizabeth Hungerford (d. 1554). (*Iris Hardwicke*)

France and was given the Garter for his loyalty, but he probably fell at the battle of Chastillon in 1453.

These were the leaders; their men, willing or reluctant, are less easy to trace. An expedition to France under Edward IV in 1475 proved unfortunate for Roger Wylly of Tenby, for he was taken prisoner and held to ransom. The money was evidently handed over by Watkyn Dolyng, a Taunton merchant. Wylly seems to have tried to suggest that Dolyng had put the money into his own pocket, but was forced to confess in 1480 at Taunton, before the ecclesiastical authorities, that the money, 100 crowns as the first instalment and £25 13s. 4d. of the remainder, had been duly paid.

Home defence was clearly safer, but no less onerous. Commissions of array were issued for almost every crisis, and in 1377 a system of beacons was established to warn against enemy invasion. Henry V's campaign in Normandy in 1415 and again in 1418 put particular strains on defence, and even the clergy were summoned to resist, as the royal chancery declared, 'the malice of the enemies of the realm and church of England'. The 'able and fencible' clergy were thus arrayed, and Bath and Wells diocese produced 60 fully armed men, 830 archers, and 10 hoblars in 1415, and slightly fewer in 1418.

Shipping could be impressed at any time. One ship and 15 men from Bridgwater took part in the expedition which ended victoriously at Crecy. In 1374, 54 seamen were taken from the port to serve on the 170-ton Bridgwater vessel the *St Marie* in the royal fleet forming at Plymouth; in the next year she went down in the disaster at Bourgneuf Bay, and the *St Marie* of Dunster went down with her.

At home, too, the royal purveyors could do their worst. In 1402 Richard Bretell went to Brentmarsh claiming to have the king's commission, and relieved the locals of cash and food worth £10. Thomas Gese, a Wells baker, found himself defending Cardiff castle when it fell about the same time, but his commercial instinct came to the fore. He bought a small boat from the rebels, loaded it with lead and metal vessels amounting 'to a great price and value', together with six great wax tapers, and brought them home. He and the boat were arrested at Biddesham, but overnight both he and the contents vanished into the mists. Perhaps more serious were the accusations against Sir William Bonville, John Frome, Sir Thomas Brooke, and Sir Peter Courtenay, commissioned in 1406 to find supplies for the army in Wales. Two years later, when two of them were dead, they were accused of raising 233 quarters of oats, 102 quarters of wheat, 30 quarters of beans, 29 'tonells' of ale, and 7 'tonells' of wine, the whole costing £132. There was said still to be cash in hand, and one William Corewyll had to explain how he had been given cash for wine, ale, and

Badge of Bishop Beckington (beacon and tun)

Seal of the reeves of Bridgwater

corn. He claimed he brought them to the late John Frome at Bridgwater, and that they were loaded into Thomas Somer's boat *le Cog John,* and delivered to the earl of Somerset, the bishop of Bath and others at Carmarthen. The Exchequer eventually accepted that story, but wanted to know what had happened to a further £16 which he had been given.

Military service, taxation and occasional oppression were the lot of many during the Middle Ages, and direction of labour was not uncommon. But in a society where many were tied for life to lord and land, such direction was freedom. Somerset masons were sent to build the castle at Aberystwyth in 1283-4; Simon the Armurer, Heremann the German, and others, the king's Devon miners, were sent to search for silver at Dulverton and Brushford in 1312. Here were perhaps welcome opportunities of changed horizons. What new skills and styles might craftsmen not bring back, to use in manor house and parish church? What new words and phrases might they not adopt or share while serving king and country overseas?

Bishop Ralph of Shrewsbury, Wells cathedral

34

IV   Exploiting the Land

Domesday Book demonstrates quite clearly that the riches of Somerset lay in its soil, and the history of the county until the present day is a continuous story of the development of its agriculture. Variety of terrain produced many different farming patterns. Down in the south, on the fertile soils around Ilchester, Yeovil and Crewkerne, the traditional open fields proved efficient and long-lived, and the pattern of strips and furlongs is still to be seen in Shepton Beauchamp, Barrington and Stoke sub Hamdon. Medieval custumals, outlining in detail the holdings on a manor, often reveal the landscape and its people in remarkable detail. At Brympton D'Evercy, on the rich Yeovil Sands, the village in 1343 was surrounded by three common arable fields, four pieces of meadow, four little pastures let for grazing, and another pasture planted with oak trees. The lord's home farm, the demesne, measured 165 acres. There were 10 tenant farmers each with a few acres of his own, 10 cottagers, one of whom was the village blacksmith, and 20 peasant families, some with 30 acres, some with only 15, who in return made hay, ploughed, sowed and harvested on the lord's farm, paid specified rents and served when chosen as reeve, drover, or domestic servant.

The apple thieves, Wells cathedral

Brympton lay in arable country, growing mostly wheat, but also a few acres of oats, beans and peas. The home farm could only support a few animals—12 oxen for ploughing, a bull, six cows and their calves—and a hundred sheep fed on the fallow arable. Over in the west, in Stogumber parish, the manor of Rowden was in different country. Already by 1307 there was only a furlong or two of arable, in an area which had, perhaps, never had strip fields; most of the land was in closes, marked out by several of the tenants whose duties involved making the earth banks so typical of the Brendons and Exmoor. The survey of Rowden which has survived was not concerned with crops, but records how many fields had recently been improved with marl.

On the prior of Winchester's rich manor of Bleadon, on the edge of the Levels where the Mendips stretch out towards the sea, grassland dominated the economy, and 10 small farmers paid extra rent for a guarantee of grazing elsewhere should the common pasture be flooded by sea water. Wheat, oats, beans and peas were grown there, the standard crops of medieval England, but this was primarily grazing land which stretched from the top of the Mendips to the low-lying moors, and detailed customs bound the smaller tenants to the care of sheep and cows.

Custom everywhere governed the life of the countryside, regulating farming by the feasts of the Church in bewildering variety, but giving each tenant of the manor a settled and defined part in society. On the manor of Stoke sub Hamdon in 1287 Walter Vox was tenant of about 15 acres of land scattered in the fields of the parish. His many duties on the farm of his landlord, Lady Cecily Beauchamp, included ploughing and harrowing in the winter, taking carts for brushwood or timber to Marston Magna, Hatch Beauchamp or Merrifield, fetching salt and herrings once a year from Lyme, and seed from Shepton Mallet or Marston. There was some harrowing to be done in the spring, but more important was haymaking, done in the 22 days between the Nativity of St John the Baptist (24 June) and the Feast of St Peter's Chains (1 August)—mowing five swathes in one or two meadows and six in others, all before dinner time, in return for taking for himself a truss of hay as large as he could carry. If the corn should be ripe on St Peter's Chains, Walter and other tenants like him were to begin the harvest, cutting three acres of winter corn first and then five of spring corn, and so on every day until it was finished and carted and stacked until Michaelmas.

William de Mora of the tithing of Holway in the bishop of Winchester's manor of Taunton worked for the bishop one day in every week except Christmas, Easter and Pentecost, and in autumn daily while the harvest lasted, labouring from sunrise until midday. He had to be prepared to take corn to Topsham in Devon, Bridgwater, Langport, or Ilchester, and to fetch wine from Exeter, Topsham, or Bridgwater. He was to carry firewood to Taunton Castle at Christmas, and when the bishop travelled from Taunton to Winchester he was to help carry his goods as far as Rimpton, on the county boundary. On the same manor, but in the tithing of Galmington, lived Robert Wylle, who by custom carried letters for the bishop wherever he might be ordered.

At Capton in the Brendons tenants by 1307 were responsible for carrying grain after threshing to Bawdrip, Dunster, Watchet, or elsewhere within 15 leagues, and were to fetch herring and salt either from Lyme or Exeter. Bleadon was in a different market area, and Gilbert Huppehull and his fellow tenants went regularly to markets at Bristol, Wells, Priddy, and Bridgwater, and if goods were to be sent abroad they were first to be taken to Axbridge, there to be loaded on boats.

The Christmas feast at North Curry, as on any manor, must have been the highlight of the year. Each tenant there was given two white

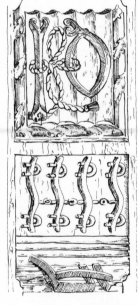

Yokes and plough, · benchend in Donyatt church

36

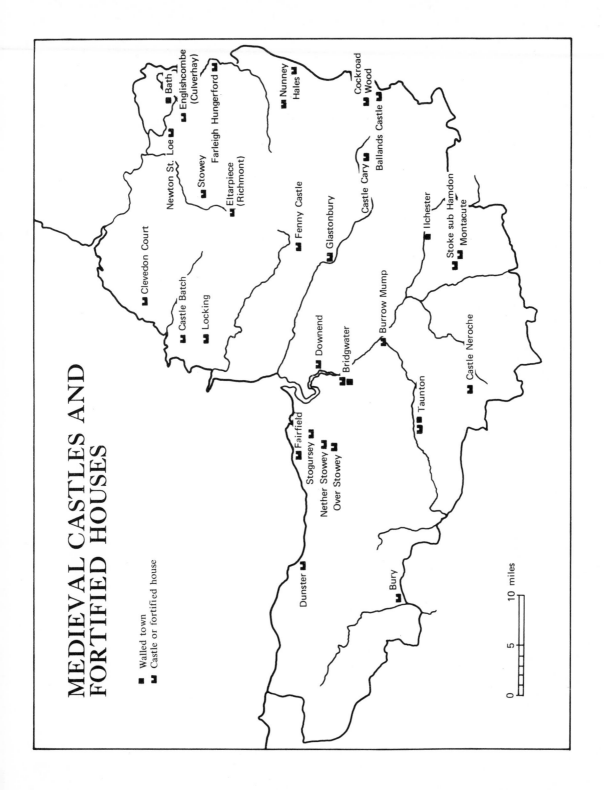

MEDIEVAL CASTLES AND
FORTIFIED HOUSES

■ Walled town
■ Castle or fortified house

Bath

Englishcombe
(Culverhay)

Newton St. Loe

Stowey

Farleigh Hungerford

Eltarpiece
(Richmont)

Nunney

Hales

Cockroad
Wood

Ballands Castle

Castle Cary

Ilchester

Stoke sub Hamdon

Montacute

Clevedon Court

Castle Batch

Locking

Fenny Castle

Glastonbury

Downend

Bridgwater

Burrow Mump

Castle Neroche

Taunton

Fairfield

Stogursey

Nether Stowey

Over Stowey

Dunster

Bury

0   5   10 miles

37

*Drinking man,
benchend in
Milverton church*

loaves on Christmas Day, as much ale as he could drink in a day, a mess of beef, and another of bacon with mustard, chicken 'browis', a cheese, enough fuel for a fire for them all, and candles to burn from dinner until bedtime. On the next day they had as much ale as they could drink between noon and evening.

Customs like these, drawn up mostly in the 13th century when the county's population was at its greatest in the medieval period, saw the land exploited to the full. Unpromising land on the Quantocks and Exmoor, for instance, was then brought into cultivation, only to be abandoned until the 19th century. Following the lead of Glastonbury abbey the owners of land in the Levels ditched and embanked to rescue hundreds of acres of rich grassland for grazing and settlement.

The prosperity which all these works brought was halted in the mid 14th century by the most virulent outbreak of bubonic plague, known as the Black Death, which carried away nearly half the beneficed clergy and probably more than half of the tenants in the countryside. The summer of 1348 was very wet, and everywhere crops were spoiled. A prayer against plague issued to every parish by the bishop of the diocese in the autumn was of no avail, and by December the progress of the disease was rapid, clergy dying and being succeeded in rapid succession in parish after parish. The bishop himself stayed on his manor at Wiveliscombe, and his letters from there included emergency measures allowing the dying to confess their sins to laymen or even to women if a priest was not available. The bishop's register also includes the first Ordinance of Labourers, the government's answer to the inevitable reaction of the surviving workforce, to sell their labour to the highest bidder rather than still to follow the old system of labour services.

Somerset was not to be affected in the 1380s like East Anglia in the Peasants' Revolt, though there were small outbreaks of disaffection. But by 1400 landowners had in many places divided home farms and let them to tenants for cash rents, so that labour was not demanded. References to the old system are still found in records of the 15th century, notably on Church property; and still in the 16th century there were isolated attempts to retain serfdom in some places: on the manor of Raddington, in the remote Brendons, officials continued to record the fact that the Davis family had left the manor without permission of the lord and was living in Exeter. Much more common was the situation recorded in a custumal of Wellington about 1600. The ancient offices of reeve and hayward still survived, and the holder of each was also given pieces of land to cover his expenses of office. One Mr. Yorke, however, had taken some of the land by 'violence and strength'. The lord's court had always in the past been held in the

38

mansion house adjoining St Laurence's chapel, but both seem to have been pulled down. There and elsewhere only the vestiges of the old system remained.

* * * * *

The produce of Somerset's arable land was primarily for home consumption; urban markets absorbed surplus produce from neighbouring villages, and Bristol especially created a wide hinterland of demand. There were, however, many remote places, particularly on Exmoor, where during the 14th century the produce of marginal land was not enough to support the small communities eking out a living in a subsistence economy.

In striking contrast was the development of sheep farming. At Domesday nearly 50,000 sheep were recorded in the county. The rapid appearance of fulling mills for finishing woollen cloth from the early 13th century tells more than the few surviving account rolls how and where cloth was being produced, but for two centuries exports took the form of untreated wool, which was sent to France in the early 14th century via Melcombe in Dorset. In the mid 14th century the best English wool came from Lincolnshire and the Cotswolds, but Somerset's wool, priced at 11 marks the sack, was equal to second-rate Cotswold. It was considered 'slight' and 'coarse', and in the 1450s its minimum price had fallen. By that time, however, only the worst wool was left. The large flocks kept by the abbots of Glastonbury or the Luttrell flocks at Kilton and Carhampton contributed to the revolution which by the end of the 14th century converted Somerset from a wool-producer to a cloth-producer. Attempts by cloth merchants to avoid export controls at the Staple at Calais were at first frustrated, and cloth producers in Somerset and other West Country areas were obliged to expose each cloth for sale unfolded, the merchants who bought them having occasionally found themselves threatened abroad with summary vengeance when the buyers unwrapped the cloths and found them damaged or unevenly dyed. By the middle of the 15th century cloth from Somerset was being exported direct through Bridgwater and Bristol, and overland through the Dorset ports to France and Spain, and 20 years later the county was the second largest exporter of cloth in England. Not far short of a thousand cloths were shipped from Bridwater alone in 1481–2 and 1500–01, probably drawn from west and central Somerset, while Bristol merchants like John Smyth did business in the Mendips and east Somerset. Smyth's remarkable ledger covering his trading in the 1540s shows how, for instance, he sold woad for dyeing to clothiers such as

Cloth worker and his tools, benchend in Spaxton church

39

John Yerbery of Bruton, and in return took Somerset cloth to Andalusia. In August 1540 he bought 38 cloths from Yerbery of the 'better sort in colores, hewlynges and light grenes which cost clere abord £4 per clothe', and exported them in two ships.

There were few men in medieval Somerset who could match Smyth, and John Chapman and John Compton were perhaps more typical. Little is known of either, but Chapman died in 1384 leaving money in his will to the fabrics of churches at Norton St Philip, Priddy and Binegar, three market centres where he had probably bought up wool from the Mendip sheep farmers. John Compton the elder of Beckington died in 1505 and is buried under a brass with his wife, dressed in a long robe furred at collar and sleeves. In his will he left the large sum of £20 to buy two silver gilt candelabra for his parish church. He gave money for the repair of several local roads, £10 to the building fund of Bath Abbey, cash to the monasteries of Witham and Hinton, and to the four houses of friars in Bristol. This connection with Bristol is significant, and so is the bequest of £20 to 17 churches, not actually named in the will, but known to his executors. Compton may have wished to appear in the guise of a gentleman in death, but like John Chapman before him, he had spent much of his life travelling from parish to parish collecting wool. This is no educated guess: for the brass roundel beside the traditional figures on the grave bears the characteristic mark of a wool merchant and his initials, marks which were stamped on all sacks which went to the clothiers in his name, or on cloths collected for export, bought from Mendips and probably East Wiltshire producers.

Chapman and Compton and their like did much of their business at the cloth fairs held each year in many villages. No fair in East Somerset could rival that owned by the priors of Hinton at Norton St Philip. There was a wholesale fair held on 27 April each year for both woollen and linen cloth. The woollen cloth was sold in the open air, in a field near the churchyard, the linen at the *George* inn. For four days after the 27th the fair was for retail business. In the 1530s the linen cloth was stored in the under-used guest rooms at the inn for several days before sale, and the owners were charged 1½d. 'hallage' for each pack. Toll at the rate of 4d. a pack was paid to the priors on each sale. Another fair was held at Norton at midsummer, and a market on Good Friday. The cloth trade continued to flourish at Norton well into the 17th century, and, as in many other places in the county, remained until the challenge from the North in the later years of the 18th century.

There were other resources in Somerset exploited to some effect. Tenants on six manors at the time of Domesday paid rents in 'slabbs' of iron, and the eight smiths recorded at Glastonbury at the time presumably imported their raw materials. By the 13th century iron ore was being dug on the Brendons and the Mendips. Quarries of fine building stone were developed during the Middle Ages, Ham Hill, Doulting and Dundry providing the freestone and the many local workings the lias or sandstone which makes so striking a contrast in surviving churches and houses. Coal was extracted at Stratton on the Fosse in the 15th century, while Priddy, East Harptree, Chewton Mendip, and Charterhouse were the centres of the four lead 'mineries' on Mendip.

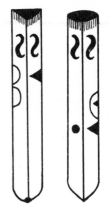

Swan bill marks, Meare; the marks of Sir Andrew and Sir John Luttrell

Natural resources of another kind have left fewer traces in manorial records. Wild life had long been the support of Somerset's population, and the Norman kings, like their Saxon predecessors, recognised the potential of a rich countryside. The forests of Selwood, Mendip, Neroche, Petherton and Exmoor, however, were closed to the Somerset countryman as sources for food and fuel, and even outside those areas hunting and hawking remained the preserve of the privileged. The importance of hawking is clear from the record of Siward the hawker, a rare survivor from Saxon England. Siward held substantial lands both in the Confessor's time and in the Conqueror's, for he was a specialist. His lands were between the Parrett and the Isle at Seavington and Dinnington, close to waterways where hawkers find their best sport and not far from wooded terrain, marshland and moor where small game and gamebirds thrive.

By the 14th century tenant farmers at Huish Episcopi were allowed to go fowling for a consideration, and Thomas Gateryn (died 1554), whose family had been in the business since that time, left to his two sons his boat 'with all manner of fishing pertenances'. The Isle and the Parrett, well known to the Gateryns, were both rich in eels. Two fisheries on the abbey estate of Muchelney paid 6,000 eels a year in 1086, and one fishery in 1475 was let for 31½ 'sticks' of eels a year, the abbot as landlord finding timber to keep in repair the weir in which they were trapped.

Landowners laid claim to the swans which gathered at the great Meare, near Glastonbury, each owner having his distinctive mark painted on their bills. The bishop of Winchester employed a keeper of swans, whose charges occupied the Tone and the millstream below the castle at Taunton and the swamp outside its west gate. Landowners also took care of herons, Thomas Tremaille of Blackmoor, near Cannington, and a neighbour ordering in their manor court in 1510 that during nesting time children were not to go into the heronry to play with bows arrows. The spoonbill carved on the benchend at Stogursey might have been a record of a local rarity or of a colony which bred there as in East Anglia until the 17th century.

Spoonbill with worm, benchend in Stogursey church

41

A parchment roll

Manorial accounts and court rolls reveal the great variety of farming practice throughout the county and the many ways in which landlords and tenants wrested a living from the soil. Always there were problems: animals straying or stolen, rents not paid, ditches and rhines not cleared, stables and houses in disrepair, mills and weirs blocking rivers. A reeve was apt to find good excuses for his failure to produce a balance at the end of the year, and surveyors had to account for any deficiency. When Bishop Ralph of Shrewsbury died in 1363 his estates came under close scrutiny by officers of the Crown, and each item returned as of no value had to be explained. There were acres of grassland under water at West Buckland, Huish Episcopi, Kingsbury Episcopi, Blackford, and Compton Bishop; the dovecote at Cheddar was in ruins; there was no grass in the gardens at Banwell, Yatton, Blackford, Wiveliscombe, Wellington, and Chard because of the shade of the trees. The garden at Compton had been ruined by the wind, and the woods at Yatton and Bishops Lydeard and the garden at Claverton were infested with adders. The bishop could hardly be blamed for the weather and its consequences, but other attempts at horticulture were evidently more successful. The bishops of Winchester had a garden at Rimpton, and in the 1260s grew linseed and flax, apples and pears, and planted vines. The gardener at Glastonbury abbey had four assistants in the 1330s, cultivating herbs, flowers, vegetables and fruit in great variety. Perhaps the most remarkable was the garden at Merriott which in 1370 included a tree nursery. The fertile soil there still supports one of the largest nurseries in the county.

Wool mark of John
Compton of Beckington

V Towns and Townsmen

While most people in the Middle Ages lived in villages, there were a surprisingly large number of towns in the county, most of them Saxon in origin. Bath and Ilchester could trace their foundations back to Roman times, and were still surrounded by their ancient defences. Most others probably dated from the late Saxon period, and by the time of Domesday Book there were a further 11 places—Milborne Port, Bruton, Langport, Axbridge, Taunton, Frome, Milverton, Yeovil, Watchet, South Petherton, and Crewkerne—which for one reason or another could be called urban in character. Some were called boroughs, implying a form of corporate government, some were the sites of mints, some had an important church, some were fortified, and some possessed a valuable market. Bath in the 11th century probably had a population of a thousand; Ilchester came next in size with about half that number, and was soon to be the county town, where judges and sheriffs held their courts, and where offenders were imprisoned. Taunton, the centre of a vast manor belonging to the bishops of Winchester, perhaps had 300 inhabitants, and was followed by the small towns of Milborne Port, Langport, and Axbridge.

South gate of Bath, 1572

Within the next 200 years more towns had developed, either as extensions of established villages or as completely new foundations. The old settlement on Cleeve Hill, probably given its defences in the 10th century against possible Viking attack, a place where coins were minted, and where the church of St Decuman had been established, was probably given up in the 11th century as more settled times came. Its people moved down the hill to the level ground by the little bay, back, perhaps, to the place where their ancestors had once lived. There, by the end of the 13th century, their town of Watchet was described as a borough. It was never large in the Middle Ages and had only 63 burgesses in 1377. Storms in the 1450s damaged the little harbour and swept away a whole street of houses, but it expanded a little after repairs were made to the quay in the 16th century, and remained a tiny urban centre, still a significant producer of finished cloth and partner in cross-Channel trade.

Wells and Bridgwater were two success stories in the 12th and 13th centuries. The removal of the bishop's seat from Wells to Bath in the late 11th century was a serious blow to the town, but Bishop Robert of Lewes (1136–66) gave its citizens a charter of privileges

43

Medieval ship, benchend in Bishops Lydeard church

and, probably long before the early years of the 14th century, their industry had made Wells the largest urban centre in the county, with a population of nearly 1,000 in 1377. To be sure, many of these were clergy, but there were others whose businesses had brought them considerable wealth. Such a man was Thomas Tanner, six times mayor of the city, who died in 1401 leaving a substantial endowment for a chantry in the parish church of St Cuthbert. His riches had not, however, always been gained by a too strict adherence to the law. In 1390 he was accused in the Court of Exchequer of evading payments of subsidy on goods imported or exported by him in his three ships, operating either from Redcliffe in Bristol, or from Crabhole or Rooksmill on the river Axe. In one year he exported cloth and corn to Spain worth £640 and imported wine, nails, and salt to the value of £359 6s. 8d. In a later case held in the same court it was reported that Tanner had in 1398 purchased cloth for £200 from an Irish boat in the Scilly Isles, thus trading illegally with the enemy. By that time Tanner was dead, and his widow ably defended herself by declaring that the Crown's case was insufficient in law since the exact quantity of cloth was not specified.

Bridgwater's rise was if anything more rapid. It was nearly as large as Wells by the end of the 14th century, and owed its prosperity to its position on the river Parrett. The bridge over the river which gave the place its name by the time of Domesday, was later guarded by a strong castle, and served as a barrier to all inland trade. Bridgwater men took full advantage, making charges for all goods unloaded at its quays whether bound for immediate customers or simply to be trans-shipped, to be taken up-river to Langport and Ilchester. By the end of the Middle Ages local landowners and lawyers were anxious to be associated with its prosperous merchants, the most powerful of whom was probably John Kendall. Kendall seems to have begun his business in Taunton, but in the 1450s he moved to Bridgwater. He was mayor and M.P. several times, and a merchant prosperous enough to have contacts with no less a man than Humphrey Stafford of Southwick. Stafford, for a short time earl of Devon, was defeated by the Nevilles at the battle of Edgecote in 1469, and fled to Somerset, presumably hoping to find shelter on his estate of Enmore or to take ship from Bridgwater. He was, instead, murdered in the town by Neville associates, but Kendall, one of his executors, was influential enough to be able to arrange the late earl's funeral at Glastonbury Abbey and to dispose of his estates.

Bath and Taunton among the old towns continued to prosper, both firmly grounded on an economy in which cloth played a prominent part. No medieval parish churches survive in Bath to compare with the

44

magnificence of St Mary's, Taunton, nor St John's, Yeovil. In the smaller towns such as Ilminster, Crewkerne, Axbridge, Glastonbury, and Bruton, the parish churches are eloquent witnesses as well to the prosperity as to the religious devotion of Somerset's medieval townsmen. The tower of St Mary's, Taunton, was raised over a period of nearly thirty years from the late 1480s. Cash, pipes of woad, rolls of cloth, a hogshead of iron and a pipe of wine were left during that period by Taunton's merchants, tuckers and drapers, contributing to the long process of construction, including the gift of lower pinnacles under the will of Richard Best in 1502, and the tracery of two belfry windows paid for by William Nethway in 1514.

There were much more modest successes, and one or two failures, in urban development, often in places where landlords tried to create totally new towns. Bishop Jocelin of Wells, lord of Chard, successfully developed an area north of the old village there about 1235, creating a wide street and offering building plots each side of it for sale. Market squares at Somerton and Montacute were less successful in the long term: the market place at Somerton was laid out before 1290 and traffic was diverted from the old route north of the church. The income from the 'new borough' thus created increased the value of the estate for its owner, Queen Eleanor, but the town's general prosperity declined in the 14th century and, having for a brief time been the county town, it sank further in the 15th. Montacute's borough still remains in name, the result of two attempts by the landlord-monks to raise cash to solve their short-term financial difficulties.

There were some abject failures. The bishops of Bath and Wells attempted urban plantations at Rackley as a port on the Axe in Compton Bishop parish in 1189, and another at Southwick, near Langport, by 1308. The Chapter of Wells tried a similar venture with little more success at Newport in North Curry, its name revealing its origins. Dowend (by 1159), Lower Weare (early 13th century), and Stoford (by 1273) were similar attempts by lay lords, only Stoford remaining to show how it was laid out in a regular grid pattern.

*   *   *   *   *

Mace, furred gown, a mayor and corporation, courts and borough constables were the outward and visible signs of town government created by charters from Crown or feudal lord. Bath had a mayor by the 1220s, elected annually in their Guildhall. They adopted the church of St Mary Stalls, standing within a few yards of the west door of the abbey church, and in 1355 endowed a perpetual chantry for all the citizens. But not until 1417, when they won a battle with

13th-century Ilchester mace

45

Seal of the community, Somerton

the priory over precedence in bell-ringing in the city, could the citizens claim any real independence.

Wells was given a mayor under a royal charter in 1341, but Bishop Ralph of Shrewsbury, as lord of the town, quickly persuaded the Crown of its error and the charter was withdrawn. The senior burgess was, however, called master or mayor by the early 15th century, and the burgesses had by then achieved a good deal of independence. Their fine civic achievement was the water supply, flowing like their power from the bishop's palace, but channelled according to their own designs in leaden pipes to the conduit in the Market Place for domestic use, and then along the sides of their main street as a means of cleansing the public highway.

Bridgwater's corporate power was organised to manage the port, and its prosperity is declared in the spire of its parish church, built in 1366–7 by a rare parish rate to the designs of Nicholas Waleys. The charter which gave the town a mayor was issued in 1468 specifically to stimulate its economy.

The men of Taunton probably had less independence from the bishops of Winchester, but their records have not survived to show how they governed themselves. Their wills, however, show a proper concern for public works as well as religious duty. Alexander Tuse in 1490 gave £5 to repair the highway from his house for some distance into the country, and Henry Bishop in 1493 gave £4 to make and mend the Tone bridge breast high. John Tose in 1502 helped to repair the highways between Taunton and Bathpool, and between North Petherton and Bridgwater.

Axbridge and Ilchester, Milborne Port and Langport had corporations whose origins lay in the Middle Ages and which survived in attenuated form until the 19th century. The people of Somerton in the 14th century had some sort of corporate status, but only their seal survives to tell the tale. Glastonbury, dominated by the abbey, achieved some independence through their churchwardens. Their surviving deeds describe in some detail their many properties in the town centre, a close-knit pattern of houses, shops, alleys and thoroughfares, a pattern still to be seen there and at Wells, Axbridge, and Bruton, and in parts of Frome and Bridgwater, but changed out of all recognition at Bath.

*   *   *   *   *

Markets and mints were characteristics of 11th-century urban life, and towns flourished where trade continued to grow. The manufacture of woollen cloth, while not exclusively urban based, provided stimulus

46

to Taunton and other places from the early 13th century, and established Bruton, Frome, Bath, Wells, and Shepton Mallet as manufacturing and distribution centres from the 14th century onwards. The trade gilds in the larger towns suggest a typical medieval self-sufficiency. Wells, whose records survive best, possesses lists of men elected freemen of the city from 1377; and by the middle of the 16th century the city's craftsmen were organised into seven gilds: hammermen, cordwainers, butchers, weavers, tuckers, mercers, and tailors, the last four all connected with the cloth trade. Ilchester, Wells, Bruton, Taunton, Frome, Bridgwater, Yeovil, and Langport supported small foreign communities in the mid 15th century, mostly from the Low Countries and France, and often engaged in the manufacturing trades. Bridgwater was perhaps naturally the most cosmopolitan town, for its merchants traded with France and Ireland, Spain and Portugal, and foreign ships were frequently drawn up at its quays. The accounts of the water bailiffs, dating from Henry VII's reign, record the goods coming into the port, unloaded either by hand or with the aid of the corporation's crane—regular shipments of wine, iron, salt, herring, coal, dyestuffs, millstones, oil, and cider; smaller quantities of salmon, pilchards, fruit, honey; rare entries of timber for arrows, caps, domestic ware, and bells.

The profits of the port went to the coffers of the corporation. In 1495 the total income from import dues and town rents came to £22 16s. 9½d. Out of that came the fees of the mayor (£5), the recorder, and others, the bailiff's expenses in going to Taunton and Minehead, and money advanced for the town's members of parliament. There were spikes and nails bought to repair the crane, glass to replace broken windows in the Common House, and locks and keys made for the coffer there by John Smith the Fleming. Gifts of wine were made to the prior of St John's hospital and to the Greyfriars in the town, and to the king's pursuivant. All the rest was spent on entertainment. John Pery of Huntworth brought a buck for the mayor and burgesses, the gift of Lord Daubeney, Lord Chamberlain and lord of part of the town. Clement of Haygrove was paid for turning it into pasties. And throughout the year there were travelling players and minstrels to be paid. Perhaps the shepherds' pageant at Corpus Christi was a local affair, and one group of minstrels came from Bristol; but there were others sponsored by the king, the king's mother (lord of most of the town), and minstrels of the earl of Arundel. Somerset's other towns must similarly have experienced something of the same rich and varied texture of life, a contrast to the more predictable life of the countryside.

*Borough seal,
Bridgwater*

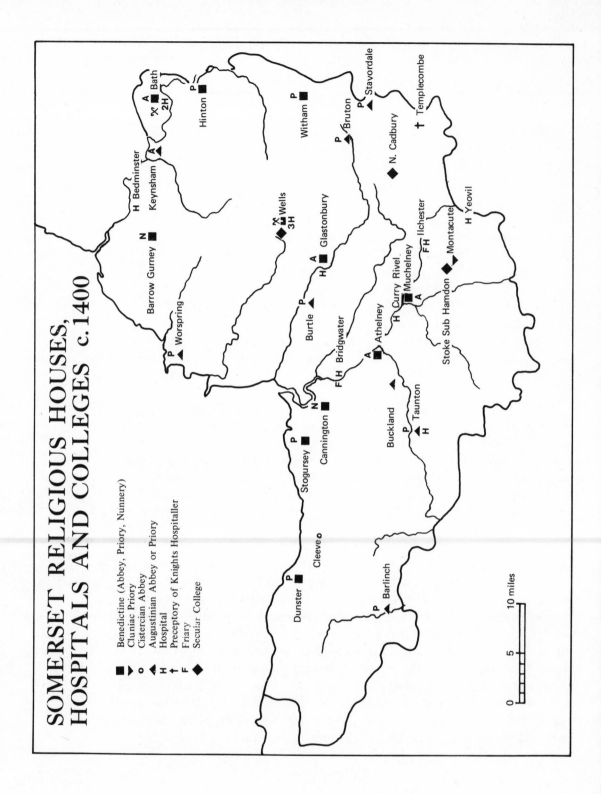

SOMERSET RELIGIOUS HOUSES, HOSPITALS AND COLLEGES c.1400

■ Benedictine (Abbey, Priory, Nunnery)
▶ Cluniac Priory
○ Cistercian Abbey
◀ Augustinian Abbey or Priory
H Hospital
✝ Preceptory of Knights Hospitaller
F Friary
◆ Secular College

Bath
2H
H Hinton
P Witham
P Bruton
P Stavordale
✝ Templecombe
◆ N. Cadbury
A
✗
H Bedminster
Keynsham
N Barrow Gurney
✗ Wells
3H
Glastonbury
A
H
H Ilchester
F H
◆ Montacute
H Yeovil
P Worspring
P Burtle
◀
H Curry Rivel
Muchelney
A
P Bridgwater
A Athelney
F H
Stoke Sub Hamdon
N Cannington
Buckland
◀
P Taunton
H
P Stogursey
Cleeve ○
P Dunster
P Barlinch
P

0   5   10 miles

48

6. The Alfred Jewel, a gilt and enamel end to a
ceremonial pointer, found in North Petherton
Parish. The figure represents Sight, and the inscription reads 'Alfred had me made'. (*Ashmolean
Museum*)

7. Gilded bronze head of Minerva found at
Bath, probably part of a lifesize, helmeted figure
from the temple of Sul Minerva. (*Roman Baths
Museum*)

18. Medieval dovecot, Dunster Priory. (*Author*)

19. 18th-century village lock-up, Kingsbury Episcopi. (*Author*)

20. Church house, Chew Magna, built about 1520. (*Author*)

21. Medieval village cross, Congresbury. (*Iris Hardwicke*)

22.   Wells: ecclesiastical city—Bishop's Palace, Canons' Houses and Vicars' Close—cluster around the cathedral. (*West Air Photography*)

23.   Glastonbury: Somerset's earliest Christian site from the air. (*West Air Photography*)

24. Montacute House: Renaissance mansion built for Sir Edward Phelips, probably by William Arnold, in the 1590s. (*National Trust*)

25. Clevedon Court, perhaps originally a fortified house of the 14th century, with additions of about 1575 and later. (*National Trust*)

VI The Faith of the Flock

The bishops of the diocese, from 909, of Wells, then of Bath or of Bath and Glastonbury, and finally of Bath and Wells, gradually established a system of government under three archdeacons and other officials which became a complex web of courts, bringing clergy and people within the jurisdiction of the bishop's spiritual authority. At the heart of the diocese was the cathedral. Robert of Lewes had in 1148 consecrated a church which succeeded the old Saxon minster-cathedral. A new building slightly to the north was begun by Bishop Reginald about 1180. The work was financed and the establishment endowed with estates for the maintenance of worship there. The building itself, agreed by many to be the first and finest example of pure English Gothic, owes much to the inspiration of a local mason, Adam Lock, who, when he died in 1229, at least knew that his conception was nearly achieved. Bishop Jocelin, himself a native of Launcherley, near Wells, consecrated the cathedral in 1239, although the west front, 'the richest receptacle of 13th century sculpture in England' was not then finished. By the time of the consecration the Saxon bishops of Wells had been re-buried in the new choir under contemporary effigies and the Saxon font served, as it still serves (so it has recently been recognised), as a reminder of the old cathedral.

*Adam Lock,
Wells cathedral mason*

Building was resumed towards the end of the 13th century and continued intermittently until the cloisters were completed at the beginning of the 16th century. The cathedral was finished thanks to the generosity of bishops like John Harewell (d. 1386), Nicholas Bubwith (d. 1424) and the Somerset-born Thomas Beckington (d. 1464), and thanks also to the lesser gifts of generations of donors and pilgrims. Their money allowed masons, known and unknown, to execute the fine designs so carefully traced on the floor of the chamber above the north porch of the cathedral, before being applied to the work then in progress. There must William Joyce have worked on his ingenious scissor arches which prevented the collapse of the central tower c. 1338; there, perhaps, William Wynford conceived his design for the south-west tower. So was created the living monument, the mother church of Somerset.

Somerset also had a long tradition of monasticism by the 11th century, and by 1200 the number of religious houses in the county was more than twenty. By the time of the Dissolution, indeed, it had more monasteries than almost any other county in England. Very

49

16th-century seal of Athelney abbey

soon after the Conquest new landowners established monasteries on their estates or gave property to houses in their homeland: the Mohuns founded a small house beneath their castle at Dunster; William de Falaise gave to the abbey of Lonlay in Normandy some land and tithes in and near Stogursey, and on that land a priory was soon established and Somerset's finest surviving Norman church was built. The Cluniacs were introduced to Montacute c. 1102 by the count of Mortain; Augustinian canons settled at Taunton, Bruton and Keynsham; Benedictine nuns were given land and a site at Cannington. The strict Carthusians were firmly established after initial difficulties at Witham thanks to their prior, Hugh of Avalon, later St Hugh, who even after he had become bishop of Lincoln came back to the quiet of the cloister each summer. The Cistercians, seeking a solitary place, planted a colony in the Flowery Valley at Cleeve in 1198, and the remains of their house are among the most evocative and informative sites in the county. Smaller houses of the established orders, friars at Bridgwater and Ilchester, Templars and Hospitallers, as well as hospitals and colleges were all to be found.

Those houses were home to only a few hundred monks, canons, friars and nuns, but their influence as centres of learning, hospitality and spiritual counsel, as patrons and owners of churches, as employers of labour, skilled and unskilled, and as landowners of vast acres, gave them great influence in the affairs of the county. The abbot of Glastonbury could rival the bishop in power, and as landowner and patron had no equal. The fame and wealth of the house was still on the eve of the Reformation a spur to recruitment, a claim which could be made for few other houses in the country. The Carthusians at Witham and Hinton still led a strict and spiritual life, but others had long since fallen short of the standards of their founders. In 1276 official visitors at Montacute found that all 20 monks were regularly leaving the house to socialise with outsiders, that the house was heavily in debt, and that some of its buildings were ruinous. Bishops in the 15th century found scandalous behaviour among the Augustinians at Keynsham, Bruton and Taunton, and debts piled up at Muchelney, Stavordale and Cleeve, where building schemes and the need to keep friends both in the king's government and among the local gentry cost them dear. Fees to lawyers and politicians cost Montacute over £28 in 1538–9, more than a tenth of its total outgoings, but dwarfed by the huge sum of £44 13s. 4d. paid to Thomas Chard, the former prior, who also received £27 16s. 4d. as prior of the daughter house of Carswell in Devon, a sum which was to cover stipend, repairs and hospitality. The only clear reference to almsgiving was 53s. 4d. in cash for the poor at Christmas, and a sum for an exhibition for a

50

scholar at Oxford. Glastonbury, on the other hand, supported two almshouses in the town and a school in the abbey. Cleeve, many people hoped, would be spared when most of the smaller houses were dissolved in 1536 because of the great hospitality it provided in that remote part of the county. In the event it was not spared but, between February and September 1536, 53 sheep and an ox were paid for by the government to continue the tradition so abruptly ended by the expulsion of the monks.

Spirituality and learning are not easy to assess in the daily round of worship in cathedral, monastery and parish church. One of the reasons for John de Villula's transfer of the see from Wells to Bath was its nearness to the houses of high intellectual standing in Gloucestershire, and the bishop's introduction of educated monks there was followed by his encouragement of a local youth, whom he sent for further study to his own native city of Tours *c.* 1100. Adelard of Bath became one of the most prominent scholars of his day, translated learned works from Arabic into Latin, and thus introduced Arabic science to Europe. And yet a man of such intellectual achievements could include among chemical formulae instructions on how to make boiled sweets from sugar cane.

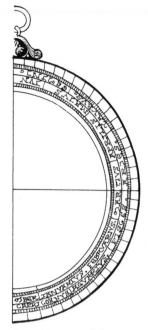

Part of an astrolabe by Adelard of Bath

Theological lectures were given at Wells in the 14th and 15th centuries, and in Bishop Beckington's time such canons as Thomas Chaundler, a native of Wells, Thomas Gascoigne and Andrew Holes like their bishop were men interested in the new humanism of the Renaissance. The library begun with a gift from Bishop Bubwith created probably the largest medieval library building in the country. The services at the cathedral were in the later Middle Ages undoubtedly influenced by three nationally-known composers, Henry Abyndon, Robert Widow, and Richard Hygons.

Learning is easier to record than holiness. Sanctity of life was recognised in Bishop William Button (1267–74) and offerings at his tomb in the cathedral not only helped the fabric fund but often produced relief from toothache. Bishop William was never officially canonised, but another Somerset man, Wulfric, born at Compton Martin in the 1080s, became an anchorite at Haselbury Plucknett. There his fame as a counsellor attracted many, including the great St Bernard. His powers of prophecy drew visits from Henry I and Stephen. When he died the monks of Montacute claimed his body, thinking to make capital of possession, but its resting place was kept a secret known only to the parish priest. Haselbury remained a place of pilgrimage until the Reformation.

But objections to traditional religion were voiced from the late 14th century by followers of John Wycliffe. The Lollard, John Yonge

Dr Andrew Holes, archdeacon of Wells

51

*Late 14th-century
guide to
Glastonbury abbey*

of Bristol, claimed that pilgrimages were neither necessary nor meritorious, and Agnes Cole of Norton St Philip in 1460 asserted that offerings to the Trinity at Bath, one of the popular cults in that part of the county, were 'but waste'. Yet the same bishop who tried Agnes was also concerned about the spring at Wembdon in 1464, and sent officials to enquire into its healing qualities and to discover whether offerings made there were truly efficacious. There were no such doubts at Glastonbury, which had catered for pilgrims ever since the 'discovery' of the bones of King Arthur and Queen Guinevere. The tablets telling the story of the abbey which hung from the nave pillars must have been among the earliest tourist guides. James Hadley of Withycombe, when he drew up his will in 1532, remembered the pilgrim centres he had not managed to visit during his lifetime—his local shrine of Our Lady at Cleeve, and then the shrines at Culbone, St Saviour at Taunton, Bradford and Bridgwater. The shrine at Cleeve was particularly popular, and as late as the 1540s a hostel for pilgrims was built beside the chapel where the venerated statue stood.

* * * * *

The beauty which survives in so many Somerset churches is the best argument for the strength of religious life, notably in the years before the Reformation. Conventional piety accounts for a good deal, and the example of neighbours created a rivalry between parishes which can be traced throughout the county. How else did the towers which rise so nobly come to have such close similarities? The wardens of Yatton sent three men in 1447 to Easton in Gordano to see their new roodloft gallery and find out its cost, and sent another man to Bristol to see some carving or painting called a 'tabylment'.

Craftsmen seem to have been available to put hope into effect. William Wynford, one of the most distinguished mason-architects of his day, probably came from the Mendip village of Winford, not far from the great quarry of Dundry, and his work at Wells and Yeovil influenced local work in style and technique. John Gryme, who made the fine porch at St John's, Glastonbury, in 1428, John Mareys of Stogursey, builder of Dunster's tower from 1442, and John Harrys, who built the north aisle at Halse in the 1540s demonstrated how skilled were the craftsmen of Somerset. John Carter of Exeter, who made the figure of St George at Croscombe in 1508-10 was brought in from outside, and Exeter and Bristol provided Robert Norton and the Jefferies family, founders whose bells are still found in towers in the county, until Roger Semson of Ash Priors began production in the 1540s. Gilbert Stayner (St Michael's, Bath, 1460), John Glasier of

*William Wynford,
Winchester college*

52

Chewton Mendip church tower

Windmill and miller,
benchend in
Bishops Lydeard
church

Shepton Mallet (1493) and John Wakelyn (Yatton 1514-28) were a few among many who contributed so much of the colour and light in churches large and small. Robert Hulle, who was paid £12 for the 'kervaynwork' of the new screen at St John's, Glastonbury, in 1439-40, was one of many carvers whose benchends, screens, pulpits, and lecterns still survive to reveal their quality and their imagination.

Benchend carvings illustrate well how religion was part of everyday life. The fuller at Spaxton or the miller at Bishops Lydeard might be donor portraits, just as the initials R.B. on many churches record the free-spending of Abbot Richard Bere of Glastonbury. The Bluet arms at Chipstable or the Hastings knot at North Cadbury might be politic gestures of a local craftsman to the lord of the manor or neighbouring squire, but the drinker at Milverton, the night watchman at Bishops Hull, the cat and mouse at North Cadbury and the courting couple at Lyng are drawn from daily life.

*   *   *   *   *

When the Reformation came to Somerset there was so little open opposition that it might be thought religion was of little consequence even though so much money was being spent on its outward trappings. The threat of legal action must have discouraged people from expressing their opinions too openly, and the only martyrs in the county were Abbot Richard Whiting, John Arthur and Roger Wilfred, who suffered death on Glastonbury Tor in 1539—and not for any real opposition, but as a cruel act of a vindictive government against one of the most powerful monasteries in the country.

But many of the underlying changes in religion had been taking place for many years. Henry VIII's claim to govern the Church was the logical conclusion of lay employment of chantry and brotherhood priests who were paid by families or parish groups to say Masses as and when required. The Protestant view of religion which emphasised the importance of each individual in his approach to God can also be traced back to similar groups in each parish, banding together to build and maintain their own aisle or chapel, set apart by screens, and providing a much more intimate and personal experience of religion.

Still, for many people the liturgical changes of the Reformation were shocking, as chantries were dismantled and the Mass abandoned under Edward VI, and as married clergy were humiliated and the Mass restored under Mary. Few, then, were prepared to commit themselves too heavily to the Church under Elizabeth, for who could see what was to come? On the whole Somerset folk were Protestant in sympathy, and under Mary people from Kilmersdon and Chew Stoke, Winford

54

and Cameley, Horrington and Wells, West Pennard and Othery were singled out for their opposition. On Saturday, 26 August 1553, the queen's proclamation was published in Wells 'which day Mass was solemnly sung in the parish church of St Cuthbert according to the old use. About this time one Thomas Lygh was sent to goal for coming into church and saying to the priest just after the second lesson at Mattins, "What the devill have we here, are we going to set up idolatry again", he seeing the picture of a cross and two candlesticks and two tapers in them on the high altar'. Thus was the Mass restored for a few years, and thus one man protested. Many more sought refuge in a State church which fined men for not attending church, forced a few who clung to the Old Faith underground, and a few others to a dour if learned Puritanism whose emphasis on preaching was for long to take the place of the liturgy for which the county's churches had been built.

Richard Fitzjames,
from his missal,
Minehead church

Ecclesiastical procession, Trull benchends

Richard Bluet and his wife, Kittisford church

VII Old Worlds and New

It used to be thought that the Wars of the Roses killed off the old noble families of England and replaced them with new, and it is true that many of those who had been active in the government of Somerset in the early 15th century—the Brookes and the Bonvilles, the Carents and the Stourtons—had a century later been replaced by others. Premature death, the failure of heirs or the headsman's axe each played their part, but the changes in family fortunes were not confined to the time when Lancaster fought York. Indeed, the Luttrells could demonstrate that although Sir James was executed in 1471 for his support for Queen Margaret at Tewkesbury, his family estates were later returned to his son and heir. Sir Giles Daubeney, whose family had held South Petherton since the 13th century, only lost his lands for a short time when he joined the Duke of Buckingham's rising against Richard III in 1483. In 1485 he returned to serve Henry VII as ambassador abroad and military commander at home, leading the king's troops against the Cornish rebels at Blackheath in 1497. Political good fortune was, however, no match for natural selection. Giles's son, Henry, by inclination fitted for military pageantry of Henry VIII's earlier years, attempted with less success a life of political intrigue and spent almost his entire substance to become earl of Bridgwater, a title he produced no son to inherit. His enemies, several very bitter, referred to him as the good earl of Waterbridge, meaning, of course, quite the opposite.

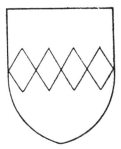

Arms of Sir Giles Daubeney

Perhaps the most tragic family story of all was that of the girl born at the castle at Farleigh Hungerford in 1473. Margaret Plantagenet, the only surviving daughter of George, duke of Clarence, became sole heir to the royal house of Plantagenet when her brother the earl of Warwick was executed in 1499 for having a better title to the throne than Henry Tudor. She was heir, too, to the earls of Warwick and of Salisbury, both holders of land in Somerset, the great flowers of the English medieval nobility. No matter how faithfully she served the king, she was the mother of Cardinal Pole, possibly the greatest personal threat to Henry VIII's throne. So Margaret perished, without trial, in the Tower at the age of sixty-two.

Somerset gentlemen on the whole seem to have forsworn national politics and their dangers, and a remarkable number of them rose to commanding heights in the law in the later Middle Ages. Two of the Hodys of Woolavington and Gothelney, Sir Richard Chokke (d. 1483),

Lady Margaret Plantagenet

57

*Tomb of
Sir John Popham,
Wellington*

of Long Ashton, Sir John Newton (d. 1488), of Sutton Wick, and Thomas Tremaille (d. 1508), of Blackmoor in Cannington, each became a senior judge in the royal courts and above political intrigue. But lawyer could soon become country gentleman: Alexander Popham of Huntworth, chief steward of the lands of Buckland priory at its dissolution, was a lawyer by profession. His son, Sir John Popham, the Lord Chief Justice who presided at the trials of Essex, Raleigh, and Guy Fawkes, invested in an estate at Houndstreet in Marksbury and other land in Wiltshire, and was buried in the state befitting a peer of the realm at Wellington. The Pophams were leading country gentry in Somerset in the 17th and 18th centuries.

The men who governed the county under the Tudors were not, however, necessarily new men for a new style of government. Wadhams and Sydenhams, Gorges and Rodneys had been in Somerset for generations. Pouletts had lived near Bridgwater long before one married the heiress of Hinton St George. The Trevelyans of Nettlecombe were comparative newcomers, for John, the Cornish Chough, had married the Ralegh heiress in 1452. Neither were the Phelipses the *nouveaux riches* they were once thought to be, for Thomas Phelips had been farming at Lufton since at least the 1460s and was living at Montacute by 1501. The Horners, too, were substantial tenants of the abbots of Glastonbury at Leigh on Mendip a century before Jack Horner was able to find £1,831 19s. 11¼d. in 1543 to buy the former Glastonbury manors of Leigh, Mells, and Nunney.

But newcomers there undoubtedly were. John Wyndham came from Norfolk in the 1520s to marry one of the Sydenham heiresses at Orchard, settling at the newly-extended house, Orchard Wyndham, which his descendants still occupy. Sir Edward Rogers came from Devon to turn the dissolved nunnery at Cannington into a country house; Sir Ralph Hopton moved from Suffolk when he acquired the site and lands of the old Charterhouse at Witham.

New or old, these families were the governors of Somerset under the Tudors and the Stuarts, often serving the Crown in matters of national importance. The Pouletts of Hinton St George were perhaps the most prominent. Sir Amias Poulett (d. 1538), builder of the 'right goodly manor place of freestone' at Hinton, who in his youth also rebelled against Richard III, fought for Henry VII, and was knighted at the battle of Stoke in 1487. One of the local gentlemen appointed to escort Catherine of Aragon on her arrival at Crewkerne from Plymouth when she first came to England in 1501, he went on the French expedition in 1513–14. Cardinal Wolsey is said to have confined Sir Amias to the Middle Temple in London for a time in petty reprisal for putting him as a young man in the stocks after a drunken brawl at

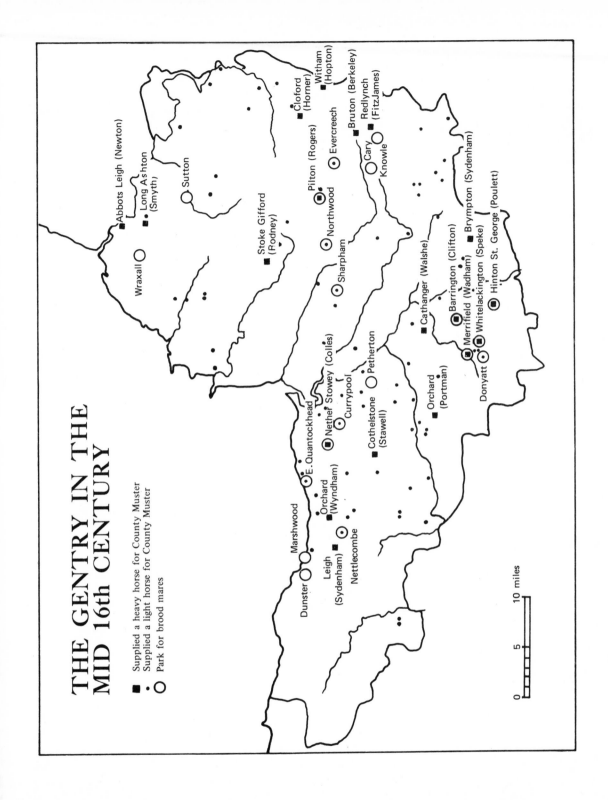

THE GENTRY IN THE
MID 16th CENTURY

■ Supplied a heavy horse for County Muster
• Supplied a light horse for County Muster
○ Park for brood mares

Abbots Leigh (Newton)
Long Ashton (Smyth)
Sutton
Cloford (Horner)
Witham (Hopton)
Bruton (Berkeley)
Redlynch (FitzJames)
Evercreech
Pilton (Rogers)
Cary
Knowle
Northwood
Stoke Gifford (Rodney)
Sharpham
Brympton (Sydenham)
Hinton St. George (Poulett)
Wraxall
Cathanger (Walshe)
Barrington (Clifton)
Merrifield (Wadham)
Whitelackington (Speke)
Nether Stowey (Colles)
Petherton
Orchard (Portman)
Currypool
Cothelstone (Stawell)
Donyatt
E. Quantockhead
Orchard (Wyndham)
Marshwood
Leigh (Sydenham)
Nettlecombe
Dunster

0   5   10 miles

59

Sir Edward Phelips of Montacute

Lopen Fair. Sir Hugh Poulett, son of Amias, served in France in 1544 and was knight marshal of the royal forces sent against the rebels from Devon and Cornwall, who in 1549 rose against the use of the new prayer book. From 1551 he was governor of Jersey, and under Queen Elizabeth was vice-president of the Council of the Welsh Marches. Sir Amias Poulett (d. 1588) followed his father as governor of Jersey, and served as ambassador in France, 1576–9. A protégé of the queen's minister, Sir Francis Walsingham, in 1585 Amias was made a member of the Privy Council and appointed keeper of Mary, Queen of Scots. He was a stern guardian of the queen, and at her trial at Fotheringhay in 1586 he urged that she be executed because she represented a constant danger to the government, but he would not be party to a secret murder. Sir Amias's grandson, created first Baron Poulett in 1627, was a leader of the royalist party when the county divided before the Civil War.

On the other side in the troubled years of Charles I's reign was Sir Robert Phelips, whose ill-written letters were for so long preserved at the great mansion at Montacute, which his father, Sir Edward Phelips, had built at the end of Elizabeth's reign. The Phelipses were more modest than the Pouletts in their achievements until Sir Edward's time, building on a foundation which had seen them in the service of the Brooke family in Somerset and Kent from the 1460s. Thomas Phelips (d. 1501) had enough local influence to be buried in the monastic church at Montacute. His grandson, Sir Edward, himself a younger son, had to make his own way. Obviously a successful lawyer, he took part in the trials of Raleigh and Guy Fawkes. Several times elected to parliament, he was Speaker from 1604 until 1611, and was later made Master of the Rolls. Montacute House stands as an obvious sign both of affluence and of political power.

Other houses in the county, often surrounded by grounds and deer parks which set them apart from the villages from which they sprang, are evidence of an emerging élite. There had been castles and fortified manor houses in the past, but by the end of Elizabeth's reign the country house had emerged as an important feature of the landscape and as a response to the changing social demands and political aspirations of the gentry. The Justice Room at Fairfield or Poundisford, each with its external door, was so placed in relation to the hall and the withdrawing chamber that Thomas Palmer or William Hill could slip away from the company to deal with some miscreant brought by the constable for examination and probable imprisonment to await the next Sessions. The impressive wings at Brympton, Hinton St George and Ashton Court, with their suites of chambers for the comfort of family connections or political associates, are themselves, each from the same copy-book in the style of Inigo Jones, a reminder that Sydenhams and Pouletts and Smyths were linked with each other not only by marriage alliance, but by friendly rivalry. The formal garden walks at Montacute and the galleries there and at Barrington were for exercise and conversation in a society with leisure at its disposal and servants to make that leisure comfortable.

Further away from the house were orchards where, as at Nettle-combe, John Trevelyan cultivated his apples, pears and figs, and the gardens where grew the plants made so popular after Henry Lyte of Lytes Cary published in 1578 the *Herbal* which bears his name. Lyte's pears, called 'Somerton' and 'Cary Bridge', might have been only of local fame, but the herbs he described for kitchen and still room were surely to be found at Nailsea Court, St Catherine and Newton Surmaville, at North Cadbury, Poundisford Lodge, and East Quantoxhead, houses where the gentry of Elizabethan and Stuart Somerset kept hospitality and ruled their county in the name of the Crown.

*   *   *   *   *

A new order at home, new challenges abroad. Sir Amias Poulett and Henry, Lord Daubeney, almost certainly took Somerset men with them on their forays to France early in Henry VIII's reign, and in the expedition of 1544 the contingent of over 200 men which Sir John Luttrell commanded at Boulogne probably included men from the estates in and around Dunster. Sir Hugh Poulett may well have taken some of his tenants on the same expedition, but John Witham of Taunton is the only ordinary soldier known certainly to have gone—first taking the precaution of making his will lest he did not return. Somerset men probably fought in Scotland under Sir John Luttrell at the battle of Pinkie in 1547 or under him and his half-uncle, Thomas Wyndham of Marshwood, in their exploits against the Scots and their French allies at Broughty Craig and Dundee.

The sailors of Minehead and Bridgwater were no strangers to the rigours of the Atlantic and Biscay, but the Bristol-based explorers of the Americas at once extended their horizons and brought them into conflict with Spain, hitherto unchallenged in the New World. In 1543 there were said to be eight substantial ships in Minehead, crewed by a total of 77 men. Four of the ships were Portuguese, and of the men 40 were away: Lady Luttrell's 100-ton ship was in London, and another was in Ireland. Trade with Ireland, France and Spain, subject to the vagaries of peace and war and the depredations of pirates, had long been the accepted pattern.

Town and port of Minehead in the 16th century

61

Thomas Coryate of Odcombe

But Somerset seamen had their share in the exploits which have become part of our national history. Thomas Wyndham commanded a squadron of three ships to Morocco in 1552, flying his flag on the *Lion,* of which John Kerry of Minehead was master. James Leach took the *Emanuel* of Bridgwater on Frobisher's third voyage in 1578, and Thomas Wiars, a passenger on board, wrote an account of the voyage, including the supposed discovery of a sunken land called Busse. William Trevelyan of Nettlecombe, who proved so much of a trial to his sober brother by his extravagance, served Drake in 1584. Sir John Trevelyan gave him 'when he went to Ser Frances Drake to go in the vyadge with him at his goinge from my house and sent unto him more by Thomas Cavell to Plimoth the iuste sume of 50s', together with another £3 and a cloak sent to William at Portsmouth. In 1594 William served, probably at sea, with Sir George Sydenham.

Almost certainly the *William* of Bridgwater was the 70-ton bark in the Lord Admiral's division which waited at Plymouth in 1588 for the Armada, and the defeat of Spanish sea power allowed such men as Thomas Gregory of Taunton to trade along the West African coast in the 1590s. Amias Preston of Knowle St Giles was on the Spanish expedition in 1595, and Robert Crosse of Charlinch went to Cadiz in 1596; both were knighted for their exploits.

Thus did Somerset men widen their horizons, and the scene was set for permanent settlement abroad. The inveterate traveller, Tom Coryate of Odcombe, patronised by Sir Edward Phelips, was familiar with the Middle East, and died in India in 1617. He was to have few imitators, but religious and economic pressures or the prospect of profitable investment made settlement in the New World worth the risk of crossing the Atlantic. Sir Ferdinando Gorges, a member of the Wraxall family, founded New Plymouth in 1628 and became Lord Proprietary of Maine in 1639. The New England coast attracted ordinary settlers like the Elliots from East Coker. Nicholas Dodge, also from Coker, founded a settlement called Block Island on Rhode Island; Richard Tucker of Stogumber and George Cleaves of Brompton Ralph established Stogumber in New Somersetshire, later Falmouth, Maine, in 1632. Richard Treat of Pitminster, one of whose ancestors had defied the manor court in Elizabeth's time, left in 1637. He made a success of the venture and was one of the patentees of Charles II's charter for Connecticut. His son and heir, also Richard, just a boy when he left home, was for 30 years governor of the new colony.

Emigration of Somerset families like these continued for two centuries and more, spreading the name of the county and of its towns and villages in English settlements throughout the world. Religious and economic pressures later in the 17th century sent such men as Benjamin Blake, the great admiral's brother, to Carolina in 1682, where he acquired 1,000 acres of land, and where he left a son, Joseph, who served the colony twice as governor. Emigration of another kind was the consequence of defeat at Sedgemoor. Transportation to plantations in Jamaica and Barbados was not in theory permanent, but many of Monmouth's followers were left stranded after their exile had expired, and remained to grow tobacco, and to leave a memory still green.

1607.

A true report of certaine wonderfull ouerflowings

of Waters, now lately in Summerset-shire, Norfolke, and other places of England: destroying many thousands of men, women, and children, ouerthrowing and bearing downe whole townes and villages, and drowning infinite numbers of sheepe and other Cattle.

Printed at London by W. I. for Edward White and are to be solde at the signe of the Gunne at the North doore of Paules.

Title page of tract on floods, 1607

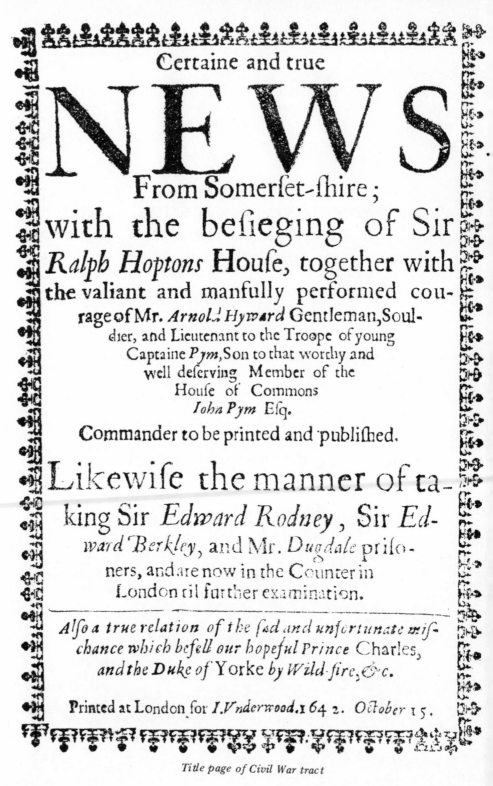

Certaine and true

NEWS

From Somerſet-ſhire;
with the beſieging of Sir
Ralph Hoptons Houſe, together with
the valiant and manfully performed cou-
rage of Mr. *Arnold Hyward* Gentleman, Soul-
dier, and Lieutenant to the Troope of young
Captaine *Pym*, Son to that worthy and
well deſerving Member of the
Houſe of Commons
Iohn Pym Eſq.

Commander to be printed and publiſhed.

Likewiſe the manner of ta-
king Sir *Edward Rodney*, Sir *Ed-*
ward Berkley, and Mr. *Dugdale* priſo-
ners, and are now in the Counter in
London til further examination.

Alſo a true relation of the ſad and unfortunate miſ-
chance which befell our hopeful Prince Charles,
and the Duke of Yorke by Wild-fire, &c.

Printed at London for *I. Vnderwood.* 1642. *October* 15.

Title page of Civil War tract

64

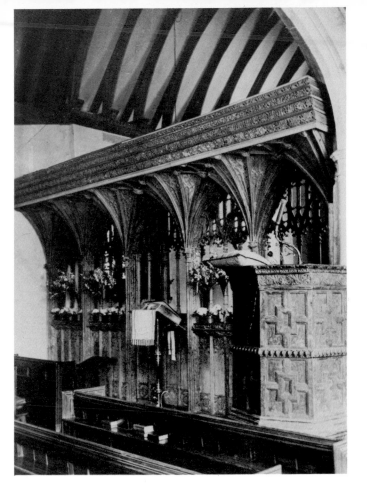

26. Timberscombe church: late medieval screen and Jacobean pulpit. (*S. A. Jeavons*)

27. Trull church: the pulpit of about 1500 with remarkably preserved figures. (*Author*)

28. *George* inn, Norton St Philip: late medieval hostelry and cloth warehouse. (*Iris Hardwicke*)

29. Former *George* hotel, Yeovil in the 1890s: 15th-century house, 17th-century inn, demolished 1962. (*Somerset Archaeological Society*)

Gatehouse, Montacute priory; built by Prior Thomas Chard (prior 1514-32). (*Iris Hardwicke*)

Manor house, Kilve, given to house a college of priests in the late 14th century. Its ruined chapel wing is often led a chantry. (*Iris Hardwicke*)

32. (*above left*) Sir Edward Rogers (*c.* 1498-1567) of Cannington; Sir Edward holds the wand of his office as comptroller of the royal household from 1560. (*National Portrait Gallery*)

33. (*above*) Thomas Lyte (*c.* 1568-1638) of Lytes Cary, wearing the jewel given to him by James I for compiling the royal pedigree from Brutus. (*Somerset County Museum*)

34. (*left*) James Scott, duke of Monmouth (1649-85), after W. Wissing. (*National Portrait Gallery*)

VIII The Civil War

The economic, religious and political differences which brought about the Civil War were as much in evidence in Somerset as anywhere in the early years of the 17th century, and Somerset men like the politician, John Pym of Brymore, Robert Blake of Bridgwater, and William Prynne of Swainswick, the Puritan pamphleteer on one side, and Sir Ralph Hopton on the other were figures of national importance in the struggle between king and parliament. Somerset suffered from inflation and an over-manned and often unstable clothing industry, and the ever-present threat of plague, starvation and disorder had been problems for many years.

John Pym of Brymore

But there were growing discontents. John Pym, a leading opponent of the Crown in parliament, found many Somerset gentry and townsmen from manufacturing centres like Bridgwater and Taunton of like mind. Protestant suspicions of Charles I's Catholic alliances and spendthrift policies were brought to a head between 1634 and 1639 when the Crown tried to levy 'ship money', taxation not approved by parliament, but charged on the excuse of a foreign invasion threat. Somerset's gentry, led by Sir Robert Phelips of Montacute and the Berkeleys, opposed the levy so successfully that the tax for the year 1639 was 96 per cent. uncollected.

There was opposition, too, in religious matters. For generations folk had relaxed after church services on Sundays, each village having a place, as at Dundry, where 'sports and plays of several sorts were used as setting up maypoles . . . dancing, sporting, kissing, bull baiting, coiting, bowling, shooting at butts, cudgel playing, tennis playing and divers other sports and plays'. But Puritan clergy and their followers declared that, like the old church ales or parish revels, these unseemly sports led to fighting and drunkenness and should be suppressed. The godly justices of the peace in the county supported the Puritans, and the Lord Chief Justice himself, sitting in Taunton in 1632, ordered all revels and ales to cease. The king and Archbishop Laud, strongly supported by Bishop Piers of Bath and Wells and the traditionalist clergy, and by Sir Robert Phelips out of spite for the Lord Chief Justice, took the opposite view. The order against revels and ales was withdrawn, and the king issued the 'Book of Sports', which declared that the old sports could still be played on Sundays with the exception of bull and bear baiting, plays, and, for ordinary folk, bowls.

But, whatever the king declared, revels and ales seem to have lost their popularity.

The Puritan view of church services was also at odds with the bishops and the Court, and Somerset provided an important legal action when in 1635 James Wheeler and John Frye, the churchwardens of Beckington, refused to obey Bishop Piers' order to remove the communion table from the middle of the chancel, where it had stood for 70 years, to the east end, there to be decently railed. For the people of Beckington, and for many other parishes, the communion had come to be a commemoration of an ordinary meal on an ordinary table, far removed from the sacrifice of the Mass, and the measures the bishop demanded seemed too much like a return to dangerous old ways. The Beckington churchwardens were prepared to go to gaol for their convictions; many other parishes submitted with great reluctance.

Dislike of financial and religious demands produced as much opposition to the Crown in Somerset as anywhere, and when the king was finally forced to summon parliament rather than continue his autocratic rule, Pym led a campaign of opposition. The first (the Short) Parliament found Somerset members disunited, but the results of the second election later in the same year were clear. Somerset returned only one courtier—Edmund Wyndham at Bridgwater—and he was soon expelled. Some members, notably Sir Ralph Hopton, Sir Edward Rodney, and Sir William Portman, were later to fight for the king, but at the beginning they were for a godly reformation. Bishop Piers and some Laudian clergy like the Bible translator, Alexander Huish, rector of Beckington, were denounced, and the bishop was imprisoned in the Tower. Ship money and the other evils were swept away.

Communion cup,
Norton sub Hamdon,
1601

But Hopton and many like him were not revolutionaries. They might dislike Piers, but Hopton would not abolish all bishops, and he could not approve the extreme measures advocated by Pym. When parliament tried to control the militia the county divided: Poulett, Phelips, Dodington and Berkeley were with Hopton and the Marquess of Hertford for the king; Horner, Popham, Strode, Ashe and Pyne were for Pym and parliament. Both sides recruited in the late summer of 1642 and the first skirmish of the war at Marshall's Elm, near Street, was a victory for the royalists. Among the towns Wells was for the king; Taunton, Bridgwater and Dunster were against him, and despite the presence of the experienced Hopton on their side, the king's supporters were forced to leave the county. The next summer, however, after success in Cornwall and Devon, Hopton came to Somerset again, and meeting Hertford at Chard formed a large and strong force which easily induced Taunton, Bridgwater and Dunster to surrender. They

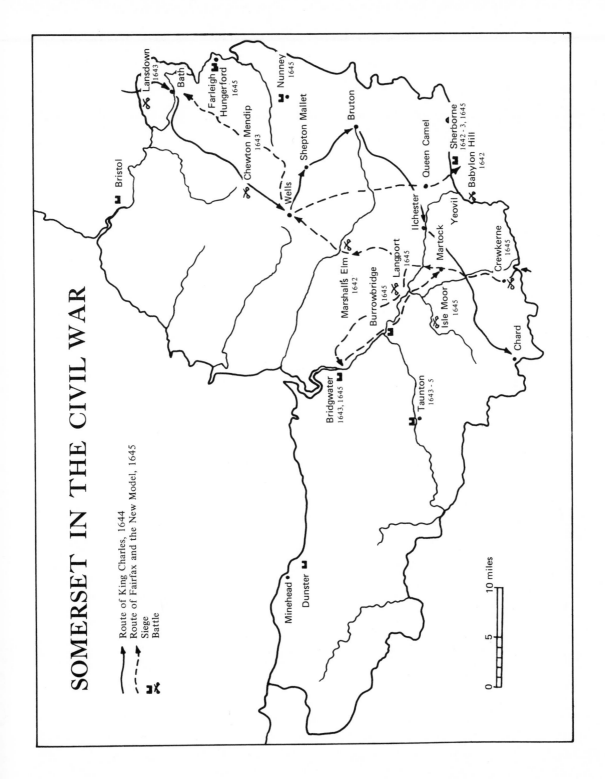

SOMERSET IN THE CIVIL WAR

→ Route of King Charles, 1644
⇢ Route of Fairfax and the New Model, 1645
⚓ Siege
⚔ Battle

Bristol

Lansdown
1643

Bath

Farleigh
Hungerford
1645

Chewton Mendip
1643

Nunney
1645

Shepton Mallet

Bruton

Wells

Queen Camel

Sherborne
1642 - 3, 1645

Babylon Hill
1642

Ilchester

Yeovil

Marshall's Elm
1642

Langport
1645

Martock

Crewkerne
1645

Burrowbridge
1645

Isle Moor
1645

Chard

Bridgwater
1643, 1645

Taunton
1643 - 5

Minehead

Dunster

10 miles

5

0

67

then moved towards Bath, where a skirmish at Chewton Mendip and then the bloody battle of Lansdown drove the parliamentary forces out of the county. Somerset and the West were again held for the king, though the behaviour of the troops on both sides was already making both parties less than popular.

Robert Blake of Bridgwater

In the following summer, 1644, the parliamentary forces under Essex tried to re-conquer the West, but the king followed him into Cornwall, failing on the way to find the support in Somerset he hoped. Indeed, in his rear Robert Blake had taken over Taunton from the royalists, and his defences of the town for three months from April 1645 not only revealed the divisions between the royalist commanders, but sapped the military forces they could ill spare. The siege was finally lifted early in July when the royalists, having withdrawn to a strong position on the west side of Langport, were utterly defeated. Cromwell called the battle of Langport the 'Long Sutton Mercy' (for he had just marched through Long Sutton parish when fighting began), and thought it was as important as Marston Moor. Certainly, although the royalists held out at Bridgwater for a fortnight, they were finally forced to surrender, and many of their leaders were taken prisoner. Bath fell, and then Bristol and the castle of Farleigh Hungerford. Only Dunster remained, but after 160 days Francis Wyndham gave up in April 1646.

The fighting was over, but the troops were not gone. Towns and houses alike were to feel the military presence as they had felt it at the height of the war. Crewkerne, on the main road to the south-west, had received the attentions of both sides almost from the beginning of the war. The royalists met near the town in 1643 and local affairs were in turmoil. The parish clerk was so involved that the registers were not maintained. Local people found themselves paying regularly for the privilege of having the visitors, and the accounts of the grammar school include payment of 6d. to a soldier 'to redeem a leaden shute that carries the water over the wall', the man having seen its obvious value as raw material for bullets. Essex was in the town in June 1644 and Prince Maurice in September, when the king himself was expected. The school governors contributed to a weekly rate for royalist army pay each week in 1644 as well as to a levy for arms. Essex came back later in 1644, and in March 1645 a party of royalists was routed and 500 taken prisoner near the town. Two months later two detachments of royalists fought each other there by mistake. Soon the school governors found themselves paying towards the parliamentary garrison at Lyme Regis, and they were still supporting the army—then named the British army—in 1648.

Everywhere in the county men suffered for their opinions both during the war and afterwards, and there were doubtless many, like

68

Clement Caswell of Crewkerne, supporter of neither side, who was 'very much impoverished' by the plundering of the troops. The royalist Lord Poulett was kept out of his house at Hinton St George until 1648, and suspicious troops were quartered in the parish until 1661. Dean Walter Raleigh was beaten up by his jailer in his own home at Wells and died of his injuries; Richard Sterne, rector of Yeovilton, was imprisoned on a prison hulk at Wapping; Henry Ancketyll, rector of Mells was probably poisoned. Less unfortunate were men like William Piers, son of the bishop, who took up farming and sold cheese in the markets at Ilminster and Taunton; or George Wotton, vicar of Bridgwater, who kept a school at Williton.

But Somerset royalists were not without hope for the future. Francis Wyndham, who had held out for so long at Dunster, and Robert Phelips of Salisbury were in touch with the exiled Charles II. His attempted return which ended so disastrously at Worcester in 1651 would have been a worse tragedy for the royalists but for the loyalty of Somerset men. Charles stayed for three days at Abbot's Leigh after the battle, passed unrecognised by the dispossessed rector at Wraxall, was hidden at Castle Cary by Edward Kirton, and then remained for several nervous weeks at Trent, protected in the house of Francis Wyndham. While there John Selleck, formerly rector of Elworthy, went to see him with a message written on paper, but rolled to the size of a musket ball, to be swallowed in case of need. He was duly rewarded, with others, when the king came into his own again.

For some, restoration came too late, or brought too little reward. Sir Hugh Wyndham of Kentsford died in 1671 at the age of forty-eight. His tombstone at St Decuman's lies over the remains of a disappointed man:

Heere lies beneath this ragged stone
One more his Prince's then his owne
And in his martered father's warrs
Lost Fortune, Blood, gaind nought but scarrs.

And from his sufferings as rewarde
Had neather countinance or regard
And earth affording noe releefe
Is gone to Heaven to ease his greefe

Sir Ralph Hopton of Witham

Sir John Stawell, a leading royalist, spent four years in Newgate prison, his estates were sold, and he himself was ruined. He lived to see Charles II restored but soon after was buried at Cothelstone in 1662 with the pomp befitting a royalist. George, his son, found the grand plans for a mansion at Low Ham too much for his straitened purse, but finished his grandfather's church there, including on its screen the text from Proverbs 24 : 21:

My sonne, feare God and the Kinge and meddle
not with them that are given to change.

George had no son to heed his warning, but his brother, Ralph, received a peerage from the king his family had served so well. He lies in Low Ham church, a building begun in the 1620s when, in a pure Gothic style, it was designed for a liturgy of which Bishop Piers would have approved.

Monument to Sir John
Stawell (d. 1662)
Cothelstone

IX Monmouth's Rebellion

Andrew Paschall, the royalist rector of Chedzoy, blamed Taunton and Thomas Dare, a Taunton goldsmith, in particular for the fact that the duke of Monmouth's rebellion was largely centred in the West Country. Some rising in favour of the Protestant cause had been brewing before the Catholic James II came to the throne, and the signs of the times began pointing to Somerset from the time Siamese twins, Aquila and Priscilla, were born at Isle Brewers in 1680. There were monstrous births in the animal kingdom, too; an earthquake was felt in Bridgwater, Taunton, Wells and Mendip caves; and, finally, in December 1684, Mr. Paschall himself witnessed mock suns in the sky above Sedgemoor.

Siamese twins from Isle Brewers on a Donyatt plate

There were more substantial signs, too. The gentry of Somerset still included in their ranks fervent Protestants who had fought for the parliament in the Civil War, and the towns were no less independent than they had ever been. The country villages in the south and west in particular, like their neighbours in Dorset and Devon, had clothworkers in their midst in considerable numbers, men for whom Protestantism had a particular appeal, 'sober and pious men' as the Independents of Chard declared, who saw James, duke of Monmouth, as 'stirred up' by the Lord.

That young, handsome, if rather shallow man, eldest of Charles II's illegitimate children, had certainly been stirred up for some time by those who wished to exclude the Catholic James, duke of York, from succession to the throne. In a movement led by Anthony Ashley Cooper, earl of Shaftesbury, a Dorset man with Somerset connections, the duke of Monmouth was encouraged in 1680 to make a semi-royal progress into Somerset, where he was greeted with enthusiasm by the country folk, and fêted by gentlemen like John Sydenham of Brympton, William Strode of Barrington, and George Speke of White-lackington. Monmouth, calling on Lord Poulett at Hinton, touched Elizabeth Parcet for the King's Evil, and her recovery only served to prove his legitimacy as Charles II's heir. A similar progress in Cheshire and Staffordshire ended in the duke's arrest, and an attempt to visit Sussex came to nothing. On the West Country, therefore, Monmouth's hopes were fixed when he was forced into exile in Holland, and the urgings of that Taunton goldsmith, Thomas Dare, found a ready ear.

Dare was just the man to encourage an exile. In 1680 he had declared in public that a subject had only two means of redress—petition and rebellion. Ten months in prison did not change his mind, and when he escaped to Holland he was at the heart of the conspiracy. While malcontents in London promised 10,000 armed supporters to fight for a freely-elected parliament and a government on the old Commonwealth lines, and the exiled earl of Argyll agreed to raise Scotland, Dare planned an invasion in the West, with a landing at Lyme Regis and a rallying point at Taunton.

On 11 June Monmouth landed at Lyme with three small ships, four small cannon, 1,500 muskets and pikes, and about eighty men. His closest advisers were Lord Grey, a few ex-soldiers, including Nathaniel Wade, whose story of the rebellion and of the treatment of prisoners is of the greatest importance, and a curious band of other men including four lawyers, two surgeons and two clergymen, one of whom Monmouth himself described as 'a bloody rogue'.

Within a few days of landing recruits began to arrive, and an army of four regiments began to take shape. Local skirmishes as the rebels established themselves and then marched north proved their strength of purpose, and the Devon and Somerset militia were reluctant to face them. The only early setback was the argument between Thomas Dare and the cavalry commander over a horse in which Dare, then paymaster of the army, was killed. Monmouth led his troops, growing in size every day, through Axminster and Chard to Taunton, where he arrived on 18 June to a rapturous welcome. Two days later he had himself proclaimed king, with the confusing title of James II. His followers, for simplicity, called him King Monmouth.

The move was not popular with some of his followers, who were republican at heart, and were more interested in popular liberty, but it was hoped that the step would encourage the local gentry to come to his support. They were, for the most part, suspiciously reticent, though George Speke sent one of his sons with 'a company of ragged horse'. Men certainly came in at Taunton in large numbers, and Richard Bovet's Blue Regiment swelled to 800 strong, but they were not skilled fighting men. Two-thirds of the 356 Taunton men worked in the cloth trade, and others were craftsmen and artisans, an accurate cross-section of the town's inhabitants, and the 74 from Wellington and the 62 from Milverton had similar backgrounds.

From Taunton the force marched to Bridgwater, gathering strength as it went; and then went on to Glastonbury and Shepton Mallet, all the time under the watchful eye of the royal cavalry under the command of Brigadier Lord Churchill, who had himself served under Monmouth in Flanders. The rebel advance continued towards Bristol, the greatest centre of nonconformity in the West, and an obvious base for a march on London. But Bristol could not well be taken from the

Silver spoon by Thomas Dare of Taunton

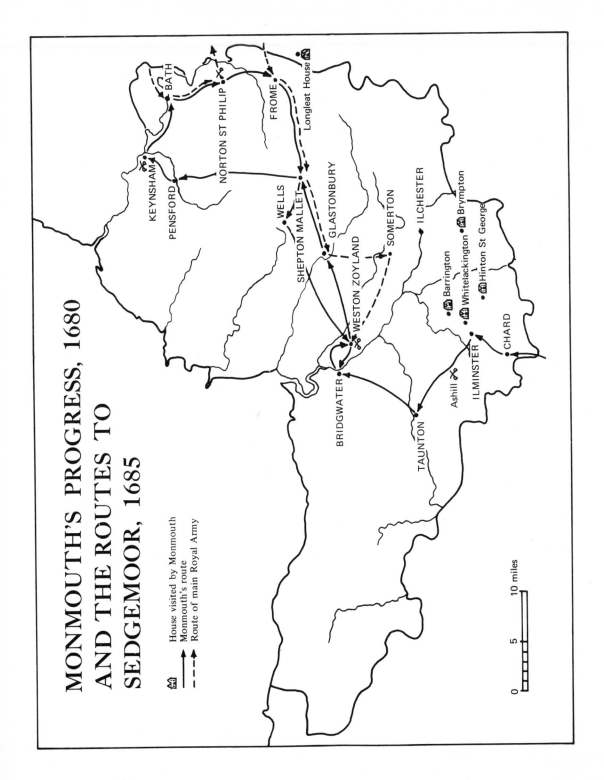

MONMOUTH'S PROGRESS, 1680
AND THE ROUTES TO
SEDGEMOOR, 1685

BATH

NORTON ST PHILIP

FROME

Longleat House

KEYNSHAM

PENSFORD

WELLS

SHEPTON MALLET

GLASTONBURY

SOMERTON

ILCHESTER

Brympton

WESTON ZOYLAND

Barrington

Whitelackington

Hinton St George

CHARD

BRIDGWATER

Ashill

ILMINSTER

TAUNTON

House visited by Monmouth
Monmouth's route
Route of main Royal Army

0   5   10 miles

73

Louis Duras,
earl of Feversham

Somerset side, and Monmouth thus spent the night of 24/25 June at Pensford, planning to cross the Avon at Keynsham. The army did, indeed, cross the next day, although the bridge had been badly damaged on the king's orders, but by that time the rebels were in a difficult position. Militia under the dukes of Somerset and Beaufort were in Bristol. The royal infantry and artillery were rapidly approaching from the east to block any advance on London, and Churchill's cavalry were ominously in the rear, based at Glastonbury. A skirmish at Keynsham in the pouring rain brought Monmouth a prisoner who revealed that there were 4,000 royal troops in the vicinity, and the rumour that the duke of Beaufort would burn Bristol if it should be attacked. A council of war voted against trying to break through to Gloucester and the Severn valley, but rather to make for Warminster and then London.

Monmouth surprised the royal commander, the French Lord Feversham, by making a night march in the pouring rain from Keynsham, and after a half-hearted attempt at summoning Bath to surrender, established himself at the little clothing town of Norton St Philip. There a royal advance party attacked Monmouth's troops as they were about to leave. Their spirited defence—very hot work, one royal soldier declared—showed the fighting qualities of the rebels. But this was no spectacular victory which might bring soldiers over to Monmouth's cause or encourage local gentry to come from the safety of their estates. After two hours the king's army withdrew in yet more pouring rain to Bradford-on-Avon. Monmouth, who could well have stayed in possession of the field, moved on through the night and the mud to Frome.

Still no forces came from Wiltshire as had been promised, and the king's army was now threatening the road to Warminster. The hoped-for diversion of a rising in Scotland, Monmouth now heard, had collapsed, and the Londoners were notably silent. Retreat was inevitable, and suggestions were made that the leaders should escape abroad. Some men had already deserted, for the king was promising pardon to those who had been mis-led. But then there came better news in the form of a man, a Quaker of all unlikely people, who claimed to have raised 10,000 men from among the farming community, who were ready to support the duke. So Monmouth went to meet so welcome a force. His army marched via Shepton Mallet and Wells, and met the new force somewhere on the moors, only to discover that there were only 160 ready to fight in his cause. Gallantly he rode at their head into Bridgwater on Friday, 3 July; and, as always not far behind, was the king's army, moving from Shepton to Glastonbury and then to Somerton, and finally setting up camp in and around Weston Zoyland,

74

a satisfactory base for operations since Monmouth's summonses to carpenters and labourers indicated he was preparing Bridgwater for a siege.

Yet his plan was quite different: he intended to cross Somerset again, this time via Axbridge, and make for Gloucester. However, a farm labourer from Chedzoy, sent by his master, came to the duke with a report that the royal army was not dug in at Weston, and that they could surely be surprised in the dark. It was an opportunity not to be missed, and at about 11 o'clock on the night of 5 July the rebel forces, approaching 4,000 in number, silently moved out of Bridgwater along the Bristol road, and reached the heart of the moor, to within a mile of the king's army, before even the royal scouts knew they had left the town.

The battle which followed lasted for perhaps an hour and a half. Monmouth's army, hampered by unclear knowledge of how to cross the deep, though almost dry, Bussex Rhine, was unable to come to grips with the king's army, where their scythes might have proved more murderous to the infantry than they were to the king's horse. Instead, they were attacked on each side by horsemen and were helpless targets for the royal guns, case shot making lanes among them. But still the result hung in the balance, and Andrew Paschall thought that if Monmouth's men had shouted they could have won a victory. But the king's men shouted first, and the rebels collapsed. Captain Dummer of the royal artillery attributed victory rather to Providence than to their own efforts.

The captain thought that the rebels lost about 700 dead and 300 taken prisoner, while the royal forces had 27 dead and 200 wounded. The villagers of Weston were later heard claiming to have buried 1,384 corpses. Perhaps as many as 500 rebel prisoners were herded into Weston church, while at least 22 were hanged immediately, four in irons. The dead were hastily buried in pits, and a week later 12 men were summoned from Chedzoy with six carts to take their turn in helping to make a mound over the still hardly covered corpses, as well as to pay their share of the cost of the irons.

And the slaughter continued. The Wiltshire militia hanged prisoners at Glastonbury and Wells on their way home, while Colonel Kirk summarily disposed of 19 men at Taunton. More rebels were found in the next few days, hiding like their defeated leader. But whereas he at least had his chance to plead before his king, his followers were cut

Westonzoyland church

to death where they stood, or, in due time, appeared in court to face the judicial murder which passed for justice before Chief Justice Jeffreys. A thousand or more fell in battle and the immediate pursuits, a similar number suffered hanging or transportation.

In all parts of the country, as well as in Devon and Dorset, families found themselves bereft of fathers and sons, their dismembered remains often displayed for all to see, so that someone described the country as looking like a butchers' shambles. It was an awful warning; and the tragedies played out in so many places were often recorded in a curious lifeless prose. Someone, for instance, summarised the whole episode in the church register of Stogursey before recording how Hugh Ashley and John Hirrin were hanged at Tower Hill at the higher end of the village and that their heads and quarters were set up in several places, and that three more were similarly treated at Nether Stowey. Perhaps this was at once a memorial to their cause and a proper recognition of their failure, for the sheriff of the county lived in Stogursey and the under-sheriff at Nether Stowey. Loyalty at St Decumans received its just reward, for the overseers paid five men generously for their service in the king's army. But who could be sure that the muskets which were kept in the hall at Orchard Wyndham and which were 'taken away and lost in Monmouth's Rebellion' were used in the service of the lawful King James? As if to declare the county's essential loyalty, one of Somerset's M.P.s, Sir William Portman, took part in Monmouth's arrest near Ringwood, and Bishop Ken was one of the two bishops sent to announce to the duke that his plea for clemency had been rejected. But the savagery of the royal retribution has become part of the folk culture of the county.

The battle memorial, Sedgemoor

X *And so to Bath*

Country houses, politics, and war, held the centre of the stage in Somerset in the 18th century, the gentry dividing their time between the glittering social round of the London season, sessions of parliament, and the idyll of a country retreat where the Classical outpourings of fashionable architects and decorators somehow blended into the rural scene thanks to the miracle of Nature and the artifice of Lancelot Brown. Add, too, the claims of Bath, where Nash, Allen, and the Woods created a magnet whose field was almost without limit, a field so much more easily accessible through a transport revolution which began with the improvement of the county's roads.

Somerset's politicians were not of the stuff of John Pym and Robert Phelips a century earlier, and yet two of the greatest political figures of the century, William Pitt the Elder, and Lord North, had more than casual connections with the county. Pitt sat as M.P. for Bath between 1757 and 1766, but the link was strengthened when the eccentric Sir William Pynsent died in 1765 leaving to Pitt his estate at Burton, near Curry Rivel, hoping he would like it 'well enough to make it his country seat'. A political opponent said he was thus changed from a brawling orator into an old apple-woman. Within a very short time he extended the rambling old house, raised a colum to Pynsent's memory, and himself designed a landscape with cedars, plantations, and laurel walks, spending quiet days out of office 'farming, hunting and planting'. In 1770 he found himself opposed to the ministry, led by his political rival, Lord North. And North was Pitt's near neighbour, for in 1756 he married Anne Speke, heiress to £4,000 a year and the Dillington estates. How often North came to Dillington is not known, but when he did there were doubtless many place-seekers like Thomas Beedall, a bankrupt Langport boatman, who was quite satisfied with fine words, five guineas, and a dinner with the upper servants—even though it gave him indigestion.

Somerset's native politicians were not of the same stature. Throughout the century members for the county were respectable Tories whose political opinions kept them out of office, the most prominent being Sir William Wyndham of Orchard. Chancellor of the Exchequer at the age of 26, he lost his post on the death of Queen Anne, was under arrest in the Tower for planning a rising in the West in favour of the Stuarts, and spent the rest of his life as Tory leader in

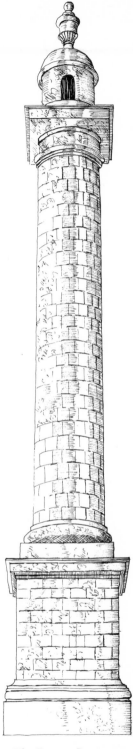

The Burton Pynsent column

77

the House of Commons. But countryman rather than politician, he was usually at Orchard when parliament was not sitting, spending his energy encouraging local trade and forming the park on the slopes behind his home, creating walks and vistas among the trees, planting woodland and fruit trees, vines and espaliers, and growing French beans and peas in his walled garden.

Wyndham's colleagues and successors as M.P.s for the county, such as Thomas Prowse of Berkley, Edwards Phelips of Montacute, Charles Kemeys Tynte of Halswell, and Sir John Trevelyan of Nettlecombe, represented the landowning interest in elections which were more often arranged than contested, though Trevelyan was returned in 1780 largely with backing by local Dissenters. Elections in several of the boroughs caused much more excitement. Bath, Bridgwater, Ilchester, Milborne Port, Minehead, Taunton, and Wells, each sent two members to parliament. Bath was both independent and respectable, returning George Wade, Ralph Allen's father-in-law, between 1722 and 1748. One seat at Bridgwater was for half the century controlled by the Dodingtons through their local estates and customs interests, and Bubb Dodington was returned ·for the borough between 1722 and 1754. Influence over the other seat was arranged between the Tyntes of Halswell, the Pouletts of Hinton St George, the Percevals, Lords Egmont, of Enmore, and the local Balches. Ilchester was controlled by the Lockyer family, firmly from 1727 until the 1770s, but then with difficulty. A London banker, attempting to build up an interest, forced Thomas Lockyer to spend £30 on each vote in 1784, and in 1789 he managed to capture a seat. Such was the state of affairs at Ilchester, it was said and widely believed, that the banker was then able to dispose of his interest for as much as £40,000. By 1800 one seat could be bought by a prospective member for £8,000, and control over both seats was acquired in 1802 by a Tory borough-monger, Sir William Manners, for £53,000.

The Luttrells controlled Minehead since they appointed the borough constables, the returning officers at elections, but they were usually circumspect, offering one seat to the government. By the late 18th century the Tudways, prosperous West Indies merchants, were the influential family in Wells, and the Wyndhams usually controlled one seat at Taunton, though 'control' often involved considerable sums of money and occasionally violence. Lord North's government was openly involved in buying off the Dissenting woollen and silk manufacturers in the town in 1781 to secure the election of its nominee, a banker with local origins, Benjamin Hammet. Hammet represented the town until 1800. North was also involved in a shady deal at Milborne Port, controlled at the time jointly by the Medlycotts of Ven and Edward

Sir Benjamin Hammet

Walter. In 1779 North, in order to be rid of one of the two members, Temple Luttrell, who had been an opponent of his policies, employed an intermediary to buy Walter's property, and then offered it to Medlycott on condition he would accept government candidates at the next election. Such a proceeding, although heavily criticised at the time by the hoodwinked Walter, was not illegal.

Benjamin Disraeli, 1834

The later history of Ilchester as a parliamentary seat revealed the system at its worst. Despite his huge investment there Sir William Manners was never certain of success, and after elections in 1802, 1812, and 1818, he pulled down houses in the town, as many as a hundred in 1812, leaving only about sixty standing. The homeless were rehoused in a 'workhouse' where as lodgers they were unable to vote. Manners threatened even the remaining voters, and said he was prepared even to pull down the 'workhouse'. The threats were necessary because another borough-monger, this time the Whig, Lord Darlington, had entered the contest. In 1818–19 he put up 38 cottages just outside the town, and perhaps as many as sixty inside. Darlington's candidates, not surprisingly, won the next two elections. Thereafter Darlington and Manners, by that time Lord Huntingtower, were apparently prepared to share the seats between them, and two of Darlington's candidates voted for the Reform Bill which in 1832 put an end to such venality. After that date Milborne Port, Ilchester and Minehead lost both members; Frome gained one; and the county returned four men instead of two. For the rest the new borough members were not to be the tools of a local family or financier, and were to be elected not by curious and clearly undemocratic custom so open to abuse, but by a uniform electorate, the respectable, middle class, £10 householder. The Reform Bill itself was the cause of widespread riots in Somerset as elsewhere, but neither riots nor the opposition of the House of Lords could stem the tide of progress, just as Dame Partington, in Sydney Smith's memorable phrase in a speech at the Castle Hall in Taunton, could not stem the storm tide at Sidmouth with her mop. Yet the reformed electorate of Taunton did not see fit in 1835 to give sufficient support to a young radical dandy who was standing for parliament for the fourth time. Instead he found a seat at High Wycombe, and Taunton missed the distinction of calling Mr. Disraeli its honourable member.

*   *   *   *   *

Somerset men fought on land and sea in the wars of the 18th century, and Somerset bellringers celebrated their victories with liberal allowances of sugar loaf and cider. The 13th Regiment of Foot,

Soldier in Pulteney's (13th) Foot, 1742

created in 1685 to guard prisoners taken at Sedgemoor, fought under Marlborough in Holland, secured and later defended Gibraltar, distinguished itself at Dettingen and Fontenoy, and after garrisoning Minorca between 1769 and 1776 returned to Wells where in 1782 it became the 1st Somersetshire Regiment. In the Revolutionary War it served in the West Indies, Ireland and Egypt. Somerset men were press-ganged or accepted the king's shilling like any others, and in the crisis of the 1790s parishes had to find money for a bounty for volunteers.

Among the men who fought in the American War of Independence were Major John Dyke Acland of Pixton, who commanded a brigade of Grenadiers and was wounded and taken prisoner at Saragota, and John Wimbridge of Curry Mallet, purveyor to the forces in Spain and Portugal, who died in 1809, his death caused by the fatigues on the march to Corunna. Somerset men, as befits a maritime county, were more successful at sea. Admiral George Rodney, victor of the battle of the Saints in 1782, was created Baron Rodney of Rodney Stoke in recognition of his Somerset origins. Following him were the remarkable Hoods of Butleigh. Samuel and Alexander, sons of the Reverend Samuel Hood, were each raised to the peerage (as Viscount Hood and Viscount Bridport of Cricket St Thomas) for their distinguished naval services. William Cooper and Alexander Litson, among thousands of lower ranks, each accepted £25, as bounty raised by Lydiard St Lawrence and its neighbours, and joined the navy in 1795.

Yet the wars and politics of Europe were remote from most people until the end of the century when the excesses of the French Revolution brought fears that England might be affected. Abbé Barbay, once a canon of Lisieux, but living in exile in Nether Stowey, was testimony to the horrors perpetrated across the Channel. And living in the same village for a time was a young couple whose liberal views and behaviour caused the greatest suspicion. The poet Coleridge was described as a 'Democratic Libertine', and his wife as a 'Democratic Hoyden' by the Tory parson of Over Stowey; and many thought the midnight walks of Coleridge with William and Dorothy Wordsworth, then staying at Alfoxton, were anything but innocent rambles, and they might well have been spying on behalf of Revolutionary France. Fortunately, there were others, like Vicar Newton of Old Cleeve, the curate of Nether Stowey, and, of course, Tom Poole, who saw them for what they were, and thus made no small contribution to national literature by their welcome.

Yet the fear of France was well founded. 'A great revolution once more in France. That rascal Buonaparte is returned from Egypt, having stolen away from the army and left 'em to old Nick. Some say that

80

35. Chilton Polden church about 1870 before rebuilding in 1888-9; photograph by Robert Gillo of Bridgwater. (*Somerset County Library*)

36. Ditcheat church, 1923. (*Somerset County Library*)

37. Tarr Steps, the clapper bridge across the Barle; probably medieval in origin. (*Somerset County Council*)

38. Peat cutting near Meare. (*Somerset County Council*)

39. Claverton Manor, built in 1819-20 by Sir Jeffry Wyatville and since 1961 the home of the American Museum in Britain. (*Iris Hardwicke*)

40. Tintinhull House; the early 18th-century front added to Andrew Napper's farmhouse. (*National Monuments Record*)

41. Watchet harbour; from an engraving by George Cooke after a painting by J. M. W. Turner. *Somerset County Library*

42. Brympton D'Evercy in the early 18th century; after J. Kip. (*Somerset Archaeological Society*)

he means to declare in favour of Royalty but he is too great a scoundrel for that. However they have made him Captain-General of all the forces and in short the Dictator. The Directory is set aside . . .' So Parson Holland confided to his diary in 1799. And as the threat of invasion grew, John, 4th Earl Poulett, Lord-Lieutenant of the county, was moved to action. Already in 1794 he had raised the Somerset Fencible Cavalry and become their leader. In 1803 he became colonel of the 1st (East) Somerset Militia, both drawn from local people as part-time defenders of their homeland. Then, on the last day of December 1803, he issued instructions to his deputies in each division of the county, which made clear that invasion was imminent.

> If an Enemy should land upon our Shores, every possible Exertion should be made immediately to deprive him of the means of Subsistence.
>
> The Navy will soon cut off his Communications with the Sea; the Army will confine him on Shore, in such a Way as to make it impossible for him to draw any Supplies from the adjacent Country.—In this Situation he will be forced to lay down his Arms, or to give Battle on disadvantageous Terms.
>
> But if unforeseen and improbable Circumstances should enable him to make some Progress at first, a steady Perseverance in the same System will encrease his Difficulties at every Step; sooner or later he must inevitably pay the Forfeit of his Temerity.
>
> How much the Accomplishment of this Object will be facilitated by driving away the Live Stock, and consuming, or in Case of Absolute Necessity, destroying all other Means of Subsistence, in those parts of the Country which may be in imminent Danger of falling into his Possession, is too evident to need any Discussion.

And so, a superintendent appointed in each parish in the emergency was directed to make a survey of all live and dead stock in his parish for future indemnification should they be lost, and each tything man was to list men willing to serve, to find millers able to produce extra flour, and secure the offer of horses, vehicles and livestock. Thirty-one men at Dowlish Wake were prepared to serve, but had no arms; the miller could produce no more flour unless rain came, and horses and vehicles were not forthcoming.

At the same time all was in train to drive livestock to safety. The details of Somerset's plans have not been found, but the farmers of north Devon were ready either to drive their cattle to Dartmoor should the French land in the east, or bring them into Somerset, to the rich grasslands below Somerton, whence they would eventually be taken to London. But the invasion did not take place, for the enemy fleet never achieved command of the sea, and was finally shattered at Trafalgar.

Cavalryman of the Frome Selwood Volunteers, 1802

Ralph Allen of Bath

News came (wrote Parson Holland on 6 November) full of Buona-parte's exaggerated boasting of success over the Austrians and the important news of Lord Nelson's victory over the combined fleets . . . off Cadiz . . . but what has struck a damp on the whole is the death of the Gallant Nelson . . .

* * * * *

And standing aloof, almost above politics and war, was Bath. Celia Fiennes had not been impressed in the 1680s, finding its houses 'indifferent' and the baths making the town unpleasant, 'the air thicke and hot by their steem'. Even so the bathers, the better sort dressed in stiff yellow canvas which did not reveal their shape in the water, were escorted by guides to and from their lodgings, the whole business controlled by a sergeant who kept spectators in order. Order, particularly social and architectural order, was the secret of Bath in the 18th century as much as the healing properties of its waters; order established by Richard Nash, 'Beau' Nash, who came to the city in 1702, and soon established himself there as the arbiter of elegance, Bath's Master of Ceremonies. With the medical advice of Dr. William Oliver, the business acumen of Ralph Allen, and the architectural achievements of the two John Woods, Nash created at Bath the social centre of the fashionable world.

Elegant terraces, squares and crescents rose to provide lodgings for folk who came to bathe and gamble, to attend balls and routs, and generally to be entertained in surroundings created by the Woods, Thomas Attwood, Robert Adam and Thomas Baldwin, the leading architects of the day. This was the world of Sheridan and Smollett and Jane Austen, the place where the famous and the fashionable came as much for entertainment as for cure. Plaques on houses in the centre of the city and memorials in the Abbey record their names; the elegance they sought still survives.

But Bath could not have been the great attraction, especially to those from London, without a vast improvement in communications. For generations the principal road from London to the West Country hardly touched Somerset at all, passing only through Wincanton, Yeovil, Crewkerne and Chard in the extreme south. It was the main route of the posts from London to Exeter and beyond, and in the early 17th century Thomas Hutchins, the postmaster at Crewkerne, was the first man to make any part of the postal system profitable. In 1677 the western post route had stages at Crewkerne and Chard, and the Bristol route served Frome along a by-post from Marlborough. The first cross-post in the county linked Bristol with Exeter via Bridgwater and Taunton.

18th-century postmark

82

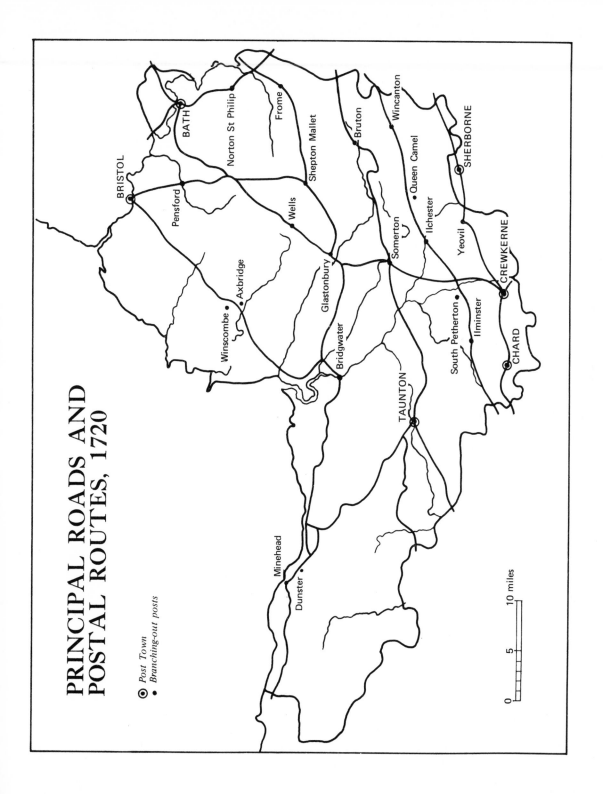

PRINCIPAL ROADS AND
POSTAL ROUTES, 1720

⊙ *Post Town*
• *Branching-out posts*

BRISTOL

BATH

Norton St Philip

Frome

Shepton Mallet

Bruton

Wincanton

SHERBORNE

Pensford

Wells

Queen Camel

Ilchester

Yeovil

CREWKERNE

Somerton

Axbridge

Glastonbury

Winscombe

Bridgwater

South Petherton

Ilminster

CHARD

TAUNTON

Minehead

Dunster

10 miles

0   5

Turnpike trust boundary stone

The main routes within the county can be traced by the late 17th century from the road maps of William Ogilby and from a fascinating survey of inns and stabling undertaken for military purposes after the Monmouth scare had revealed shortcomings in the army's communications system. Towns on the main roads offered plenty of accommodation for both men and horses, while smaller places on frequented roads were simply provided with ample stabling for changing horses. Chard thus had 91 beds and stabling for 342; Crewkerne 54 beds and stabling for one hundred and thirty. Wincanton had fewer inns and only 50 beds, but its stables could take 254 horses. Wells, still the largest town in the county, offered 492 beds and stabling for 599, followed by Bath, Taunton and Bridgwater. Pensford, a small village on the Bristol Road, and Bishops Lydeard, still not a town, were both remarkably well endowed with inns, the former with 60 beds, the latter with only 20, but with room for 102 horses.

Apart from the main London-Exeter route, the principal east-west roads in the early 18th century were through Castle Cary, Somerton and Taunton towards Exeter; or through Frome, Shepton Mallet, Glastonbury and Bridgwater, and thence either to Taunton or over the Quantocks to Minehead. The two roads south and south-west of Bristol were neither ideal: the way between Axbridge and Bridgwater was often impassable in winter along the undrained flats of the Parrett, and of the two routes south of Wells, the direct way over the Mendips involved the steep hill at Dundry where extra horses were needed for heavy loads. A new east-west route was canvassed in the 1760s from London via Andover to Wincanton, Somerton, Langport, and Taunton. The route had the support of influential Wiltshire figures like Alderman Beckford and Mr. Hoare, the banker, and Lord Chatham was asked by the sponsors for his encouragement, which they hoped would be forthcoming since the route passed in front of his house at Burton Pynsent. The idea came to nothing, but a similar route was established in the early 19th century from Andover and Wincanton through Ilchester, the foundation of the popular A303. One of the sponsors of that route was Sir William Manners, whose interest was less in the improved journey than in the safety of his parliamentary seat at Ilchester.

Regular maintenance of even major roads was until the 18th century the responsibility of the parishes through which they passed, and under such circumstances any general improvement was unlikely. The creation of turnpike trusts allowed stretches of road to be maintained instead by local bodies who could raise money for the purpose and charge travellers for the use of the road. In Somerset the Bath Trust was formed in 1707-8, and another, based on Bristol, in 1731. From 1753 most of the county's principal roads were maintained in such a way, and the consequent improvements were obvious. Entirely new lines of road were created to avoid steep hills, new bridges and causeways were built, and some old routes, like the Great Road across the Quantocks between Nether Stowey and West Quantoxhead, were virtually abandoned. From 1816 the road surfaces themselves were vastly improved by the work of J. L. Macadam, who first advised the Bristol and Bath trusts in 1815–16, and who, with his family, dominated the Somerset road system in the 1820s and 1830s.

Improved communications demanded improved facilities en route, and every inn worth the name, like the *Lovington* inn on the Somerton-Castle Cary road (now Brue Farm), or the *George* inn at Crewkerne, on the Exeter road, was extended around a yard where fresh horses were always ready for the next stage of the travellers' journey. Coaches and carriers, often organised if not owned by enterprising innkeepers, plied between towns, vying with each other for speed, often at the risk of their passengers or goods, and the importance of such routes to the towns themselves was considerable. The great brick stable block at Barrington Court, built in 1674, Sir William Portman's 11 'house' horses and seven coach horses at Orchard Portman in 1690, and the five coach houses and stabling for 25 horses at Burton Pynsent are but three examples of the way the more prosperous organised their journeys from place to place.

Whatever the state of the roads, news travelled fast enough, and Dr. Claver Morris of Wells (1659–1726) made a good living as a doctor whose practice stretched into Wiltshire and Gloucestershire in the east and to Exeter in the west. Wet weather was the great hazard for those for whom speed was essential, or a heavy load a responsibility. Young Gapper, a Somerton doctor's apprentice, took a risk when he carried off Ann Virgin's daughter in a chaise from Langport in October 1768. Other eloping couples used the London-Exeter road for speed, and found the isolation of the little church at Cricket St Thomas, hidden from view by the hillside and the trees, entirely suitable for their clandestine weddings.

The Lovington inn

The improvements effected by turnpikes were real, and were to last until the motorway movement of the 1970s brought the M5 snaking inexorably if elegantly through the county. In December 1800 the Staniforth family of Liverpool, travelling from Cornwall, commented on the 'very good' road through the county, and their progress bore witness to its quality. They left Exeter at 9 o'clock one Monday morning, changed horses at Cullompton, at the *Castle* in Taunton and at the *King's Head* in Bridgwater, and reached the 'clean and comfortable' *Piper's* inn at 6 o'clock after a journey of 40 miles. They left there at 9 the next morning, but the weather was too wet to allow them to leave their coach at Glastonbury. They changed horses at the *Swan* at Wells and stayed long enough to visit the cathedral, but found the next stage to Bath rather long, for no horses were available at the *Old Down* inn. They arrived at the *White Hart* at Bath at 3, a leisurely six hours for 30 miles; entirely satisfactory.

Nether Stowey
turnpike house

XI Land, Labour and Learning

John Billingsley, of Ashwick Grove, near Shepton Mallet, one of the county's leading agriculturists, declared in his detailed survey of Somerset's farming in 1795 that not enough grain was grown there for the needs of its people, but that if the vast areas of marsh, waste and common field were drained and enclosed, and then improved with proper management rather than farmed by the traditional methods, then the county could be self-sufficient and the value of the new lands at 30 years' purchase would increase by six million pounds. In the 1760s a visitor noted how on the Levels north and north-east of Bridgwater the only worthwhile stock were the black West Devon or Cornish cattle, since the local beasts were heavy, sluggish and unshapely, producing soft and spongy beef. Locally-born colts, too, had to be removed to drier areas for rearing or they would become nothing but drudges in the damp conditions. Indeed, the only native success recorded in the whole county at the time were the great cheeses made at Cheddar, which fetched three times as much as their rivals from Cheshire.

John Billingsley

There were, of course, farmers who wanted to improve their stock and yields. Mr. Speke, when advising William Pitt on his new estate at Burton Pynsent, recommended 600 Dorset sheep for their wool and better market value, and a black horse and 10 or 12 Northamptonshire mares for both plough and coach work. He suggested the creation of a dairy of 30 or 40 cows, which could be let, in the tradition of that part of the county, for four guineas each a year. For the undrained acres of West Sedgemoor he could, however, only suggest the traditional rearing of oxen for plough or market.

From 1777 the Bath and West of England Agricultural Society offered premiums for improvements in machinery, stock and husbandry, and individual farmers came to be known as successful specialists. Messrs. Morgan of Woolverton, Day of Foxcote, Young of Camerton, Holbrook of Corston, and Smith of Twerton, were leading sheep breeders who had rejected the native Mendip variety in favour of Dorsets, and were taking advantage of a Spanish ram given by George III to the Bath Society. Mr. Poster, farming near Yeovil, and Mr. Lowman near Crewkerne, had brought in Leicestershires, while Mr. Jeanes of Alhampton had discovered a cure for footrot, that scourge of the wetlands which, in one year in the parish of Mark, was said to have infected 10,000 sheep.

Bath and West Agricultural Society's button

Mr. White Parsons of Ilchester challenged his neighbours to produce a Devon bull better than his own, and won. Agricultural societies at Dunster, Dulverton and Wiveliscombe among others offered prizes at the turn of the century for the best heifer and calf, and best stallion, the best bull, and the best boar. Individual farmers elsewhere were known for their own particular contributions: Mr. Anderdon of Henlade and two farmers from Halse had successfully used the seed drill in the 1790s; Mr. William Moxham of Glastonbury had turned several peat bogs near the town into fine meadows, and Mr. Walwyn of Kilmersdon had improved his grassland with the introduction of sanfoin. Landowners like Mr. J. F. Luttrell of Dunster, James Bernard of Crowcombe and Squire Rogers of Yarlington were known respectively for the formation of water meadows, the cultivation of turkey rhubarb, and the application of marl. Mr. Parsons of West Camel had become an expert in burning clay so that it could be spread on fields.

Progress as a whole could not, however, be made without the wholesale co-operation of landlords, tenants and commoners in the vast areas of moorland and marsh. Billingsley described how at Wedmore in the 1770s some 3,000 acres of common had been enclosed and drained. The many cottagers whose common rights had for years caused overstocking lost their grazing, but in return gained opportunities for work so that the value of the land had risen and the parish poor rate had not. To an agriculturist this was justification enough. The vast area of King's Sedgemoor proved a much more difficult problem. After years of negotiation an Act was passed in 1791 under which the King's Sedgemoor drain was dug through the centre of the moor, but because of opposition from the bishop of Bath and Wells, who feared loss of tithe income, the villagers of Weston Zoyland had to wait until 1834 before they, years after their neighbours, could take advantage of enclosure in their parish. Enlightened landowners like John Knight, who rescued Exmoor from oblivion and created the village of Simonsbath, were few.

Agricultural improvement was slow, and bad harvests in the 1790s, the French War, and rapidly increasing population created a crisis which became acute. It was all very well for a few patronising farmers at Dunster Show in 1800 to give Richard Hurley of Sampford Brett a prize for bringing up six children without the help of parish relief, or to give John Gould of Withycombe another for serving as a 'menial servant in husbandry' with the same employer for 23 years. These two were among the fortunate ones. There were too many in the same area of the county for whom life was a bare existence.

In April 1801 a survey was carried out among the Brendon and Quantock parishes of Williton hundred to discover what stores were

88

available to feed the poor. Wheat, barley and potatoes were their staple diet, but Elworthy had only enough barley left for the spring sowing and the overseers had brought in rice instead, and several other parishes had supplies of pilchards or herrings. Chipstable had plenty of oats, but the potatoes were nearly gone, wheat supplies were low, and only barley for seed, but the poor had found herrings for sale at Wiveliscombe market which cost 3d. a day. While the French War lasted prices rose and the crisis with it. Political agitation which followed was as acute in the country as anywhere. In the autumn of 1830 landlords and farmers for miles around Ilminster destroyed or dismantled their own threshing machines lest the 'tumult' should burn them down, and only Lord Egremont's machine at Beercrocombe was left standing. Furniture from an empty farmhouse on his estate had been removed for safety, but the neighbouring tenant wrote to his lordship asking whether lintels should be taken down, 'for theyl be carred away otherwise'.

The alternatives to violence were full of risks. Some labourers moved to the towns, only to find unemployment there was at least as bad: Frome had 557 men on the poor rate in 1831, out of a total population of 12,240. The vicar there was one of many who encouraged men to emigrate: in 1831, 85 people left for Canada, and in 1832 a further 138, all at the expense of the parish. The Colonial Land Emigration Commission employed Mr. A. A. Mullett as a 'selecting' agent in Taunton in 1842 as one among many channels by which the labouring poor could find a new hope. Mullett received £1 for every married couple and 7s. for each single adult selected for free passage out of Plymouth. The *Salisbury and South Wilts. Herald,* among other West Country newspapers, advertised for 'healthy young (and not large) working families' willing to brave the uncertainties of the unknown. From the 1840s onwards men and women in their hundreds, probably in their thousands, taking up the offers of men like John Toms, the Chard postmaster and shipping agent, sailed for the colonies or America, creating communities of Somerset folk across the world. There were Shepton Beauchamp people at Buffalo and Pittsburg, families from Middlezoy, Othery and Weston Zoyland in Lake County, Illinois, Austins from Baltonsborough in Tasmania and Victoria. The name Somerset, given to county, town and village in eight states in the U.S.A., on the southern tip of Africa, in Quebec, Queensland, and Tasmania shows how widespread was emigration from the county.

Considering a passage

Letters home left readers in no doubt that the promised land did not always live up to expectations. Emigrants might have been sent off, like a group from Bridgwater in March 1852, with a blessing from the pompous curate, but Samuel Howell, who left Castle Cary at about that time for Iowa was not alone in wishing he was back home;

but he was trapped, for no-one would give him a cent for his possessions. More fortunate was S. L. Willcox, formerly from the Highbridge district, who was living at Williamsburg, Long Island, in 1864. Exactly how he made a living is not clear, but of his two sons, the younger fought in four battles on the Union side in the Civil War before he was 17, and then entered the machinery business. The elder, a civil engineer and architect, was a staff officer at Gettysburg and published maps of the battlefields of Antietam, Fredericksburg, and Gettysburg. Somerset men were again distinguishing themselves beyond the seas.

The risks of emigration were probably better than starvation at home. In 1843 it was established that the labourer was worse off in Somerset than in Wiltshire, Dorset or Devon. The man later to be one of the leaders of the Agricultural Labourers Union, George Mitchell, began work in the fields of Montacute at the age of seven for a few pence a week. By the age of 19 he was paid 4s. a week whatever the hours, working one haymaking time from 4 o'clock in the morning, when he harrowed a field of turnips, and then made hay for a total of 18 hours, all on inadequate food. Montacute was in fertile country, but only in the 1870s, when Mitchell's organised strikes in the area had raised weekly wages from 9s. to 10s., the truth began to be told. That wage was still totally inadequate, living conditions appalling. Yet a large farmer could make a fortune in seven years, for he paid so little rent to his landlord and so little wages to his men.

Cannington was in a similarly rich district, and wages there in the 1870s included the usual daily ration of cider. One typical labourer, who did not care to be too closely identified, earned 2s. a day on piece work, but nothing in wet weather. He sent his five daughters to school, which cost him 2d. a week; 1s. 6d. went in rent, 6d. to clothing and coal clubs. He had a tiny garden for potatoes, but kept no pig. The only meat his family ever ate were red herrings. The day before that man was interviewed he had but 5½d., with which he bought a loaf and a herring for his entire family; he himself had nothing to eat all day. Any allotment he and his fellows were lucky enough to get was let by the farmers at four times the rate the farmer himself paid the landlord. One family was found at Athelney for whom even bread was a luxury.

The agricultural depression of the late 19th century made the lot of the labourer potentially worse. America and the colonies still beckoned some, and so did expanding industrial South Wales. The Agricultural Labourers Union began campaigning in the Ilminster area in 1872, and at first their efforts had the desired effect of raising wages. At the Church Congress in Bath in 1873 the Labour Question found the church divided: some advocated a policy of direct support

Cider jar

for the unions, others did not want to offend honest employers. The Reverend Stuckey Coles of Shepton Beauchamp, who acted for the Labourers' Friend Society, rather sat on the fence; Sydenham Hervey, curate of neighbouring South Petherton, went to a meeting held in his parish addressed by the union leader, Joseph Arch, and by George Mitchell:

> Arch spoke about 1½ hour, with great earnestness, vigour, fluency and at times eloquence—a superior looking man—which Mitchell is not. A tolerable number of labourers present, nearly all of whom seemed quite satisfied to be left alone . . .

The Dundas aqueduct near Bath

Annual meetings of the union were held on Ham Hill for some time afterwards, and in 1877 Mitchell asked the schoolmaster of nearby Stoke sub Hamdon to teach his children the tune *John Brown* for the coming demonstration. 'Of course', wrote the master, who owed his position to farmers and glove factory owners, 'I did not accede to his request'.

But there were farmers, at least, who were changing with the times. W. B. Peren, who had 230 acres at Compton Durville, near South Petherton, was especially proud of his herd of cows. Where others before him had named only the inmates of their stables, Peren named his cows, or rather those with breeding, for he made a clear distinction between three Irish cows, the half-Alderney, and the rest, all serviced by his bull Baron Fawkes. There was Evangeline, presumably inspired by Longfellow, Roseblush, May Queen, Rosetta, Queen of the Roses, and Blue Rosette. He took Baron Fawkes, Queen of the Roses and her calf to the Bath and West show at Exeter in May 1879, but came back without a prize. However, that year he made a cash profit of nearly £1,086, clearly the result of good stock management. Here was a farmer far removed from a century before, when Mr. Speke was advising Mr. Pitt.

Horizons were changing in other ways, for the network of canals and railways which crossed the county extended the markets for agricultural products and brought even the remotest villages into contact with a wider world. The Parrett, the Yeo, the Tone, and the Bristol Avon were all in various ways improved to make navigation possible far inland from the county's ports, and a good livelihood was made in the carrying business. Bradfords had been trading up the Parrett since the 15th century, and Welsh coal was brought in barges in the 17th century as far as Ham on the Tone, and from there taken overland as far as the Blackdowns. By the 1740s the Langport firm of Stuckey and Bagehot had been established, and in the 1790s they were trading regularly with Manchester, Liverpool, Birmingham and London by road and by water. By 1866 they owned 14 East

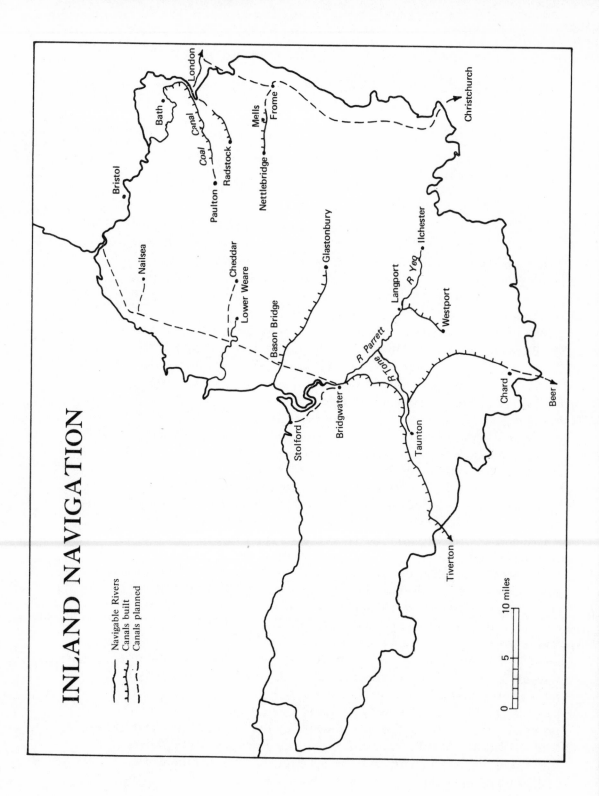

INLAND NAVIGATION

Navigable Rivers
Canals built
Canals planned

London

Christchurch

Bath

Coal Canal

Bristol

Paulton
Radstock

Mells
Frome

Nettlebridge

Glastonbury

Ilchester

Nailsea

R Yeo
Langport

Cheddar
Lower Weare

Westport

Bason Bridge

R Parrett

Chard

Beer

Stolford

R Tone

Bridgwater

Taunton

Tiverton

10 miles

0   5

92

Indiamen and 19 barges as well as having a controlling interest in a large banking concern.

Canals seem to have exercised a peculiar fascination, but more were built on paper and described in Acts of Parliament than were ever opened to traffic. The great challenge was to build a waterway to link the Bristol and English Channels. Famous canal engineers like James Brindley and John Rennie surveyed routes, parts of which were later adopted in more modest schemes. The Channel-to-Channel idea remained alive, if impractical, until late in the 19th century, when the Board of Admiralty discussed a plan to link Lilstock with Beer in Devon by a canal not only wide enough to take a Dreadnought, but with a basin along its route large enough for such a vessel to turn round.

Basin warehouse, Westport canal

The more modest schemes began with coal canals, intended to give the Somerset coalfield a cheap and efficient outlet via the Kennet and Avon at Bath to the London market. Indeed, the first such canal was a branch of another of those grandiose schemes, the Dorset and Somerset canal, which was to link the Dorset Stour with the Kennet and Avon. A branch from Frome to the collieries at Nettlebridge was to be the first stage, for Frome was then one of the most important cloth manufacturing centres in the West of England. Nearly eight miles were dug, and a lift or balance lock built by Mr. Fussell, owner of the nearby Mells ironworks, was installed. But although five more lifts were planned the money ran out in 1802 and the branch was never finished—and the main canal was not even started.

Topography was the great problem for the two other coal canals. From the Kennet and Avon at Limpley Stoke a line was planned to Midford where it divided, one branch running up the valley through Combe Hay, Dunkerton and Camerton to Timsbury, the other via Writhlington to Radstock. The first branch was partially opened in 1798, but the gradient at Combe Hay proved insuperable: caissons and then an inclined plane with a crane were tried without success, but with much delay, and finally the canal was opened in 1805 with a flight of 22 narrow locks at Combe Hay. The Radstock branch was also partially opened in 1798, but another gradient faced the navigators near Wellow. In 1815 the whole line was converted to a tramway.

The remaining canals in the county came very late in the day. Schemes to link the Avon below Bristol with Taunton, and Taunton with the Exe at Topsham in the 1790s only produced 11 miles of canal in 1814, between Tiverton and Holcombe Rogus, after four years of work, but the general idea was retained and in 1827 the first section was completed between Huntworth, on the Parrett, near Bridgwater, and Taunton, and was named the Bridgwater and Taunton canal. In 1837 the canal was extended at the Bridgwater end to connect

CAUTION.

THE Public are cautioned against believing certain statements which are abroad respecting the effects of the CANAL BILL now before Parliament, whereby the Public are told that they will be at the mercy of the Canal Company, to charge them whatever price they please for Coals. THIS IS UTTERLY FALSE, as the *Canal Company's Powers are limited*, and the very utmost Toll they can levy under their Act, is **2** shillings per Ton. Their present Toll is **1** shilling; so that if they were to do the utmost they are empowered to do by Law, it would only be an increase in price of **1** Shilling per Ton, or not quite *three farthings per hundred* above the present price.

TROOD, Printer, Bookbinder, and Auctioneer, TAUNTON

(inform you Nathaniel that the form will be there)
(uran m stock that only)

TENDER MERCIES,

INTENDED BY THE

Canal Company.

In answer to a Handbill I have just seen, headed "CAUTION," evidently emanating from the Friends of the Canal, and consequently, the enemies of the People of Taunton, I do assert, that before the Canal Company seized on the Old River, I used to pay *Five Shillings* for every Boat Load of Timber sent from my Wharf at Bathpool; but immediately the River was seized on by the Canal Company, they gradually increased their demands, and ultimately extorted *Ten Shillings* per Boat. God only knows what they would now charge had they not been dispossessed of the River! So much for the Tender Mercies to be expected from the Canal Speculators, who intend to engross to themselves all the Trade of Taunton, and all the benefits to be derived from the River Tone.—Fie on them!!

WM. YATES,

Timber Merchant,

BATHPOOL,

W. TOMS, PRINTER, TAUNTON.

Two canal broadsheets

with the ingenious new dock which had been built north of the town. At the Taunton end a narrow canal named the Grand Western was built between Taunton and Greenham on the Devon border. Designed by James Green, it had a series of eight lifts and an inclined plane at Wellisford operated, after many difficulties, by a steam engine. Elsewhere there was a short-lived canal from 1834 linking Glastonbury with Bason Bridge; the Chard canal with four inclined planes and a tunnel opened in 1842, and the short Westport canal (1840).

Isambard Kingdom Brunel

Almost universally the coming of the railways spelt ruin for the canals. Brunel's broad gauge track for the Bristol and Exeter railway snaked its level way along the Somerset moors much as the M5 motorway was to do a century and more later, reaching Bridgwater in 1841, Taunton in 1842, and the county boundary in 1843. By 1844 the line was opened to Exeter. From that date the county was rapidly opened to rail travel. The Wiltshire, Somerset and Weymouth line reached Frome in 1850 and continued through Bruton and Castle Cary to Yeovil in 1856. Frome was also linked to Radstock for coal traffic in 1854 and Frome's wooden station buildings remain as a rare survival from that period. Meanwhile a line was built between Taunton, Langport, Martock and Yeovil in 1853, and the Somerset Central railway opened a broad gauge track from Highbridge Wharf to Glastonbury, largely along the course of the old canal. That railway, in 1858 extended at its western end to a pier at Burnham, was driven eastwards to Cole, near Bruton, to join the Dorset Central line from Wimborne, thus creating the famous Somerset and Dorset joint railway. In 1874 a link with the Midland railway brought traffic along a dramatic route over the Mendips to Evercreech and then south-east to Templecombe and on to Bournemouth. At Templecombe the Somerset and Dorset, familiarly known as the 'slow and dirty', was connected with the main route from London Waterloo to Exeter and beyond, a line which in 1860 reached Yeovil Junction and Crewkerne.

Branches from the main lines served the county well. The growing resort of Clevedon was linked with the network from 1847 to take at least some of the seaside trade which Weston had recently been enjoying. Minehead was not reached until 1874, though Watchet's commercial possibilities had ensured that it was linked with the main line at Norton Fitzwarren in 1862. In 1859 Watchet had become the terminus of the West Somerset Mineral railway, a narrow gauge track which by conventional route and by a huge incline brought iron ore from the Brendon mines to be shipped to South Wales.

Wells, almost in the centre of the railway web, was joined in 1859 to Glastonbury, in 1862 to Shepton Mallet and the East Somerset railway, part of which still remains, and in 1870 by a track from

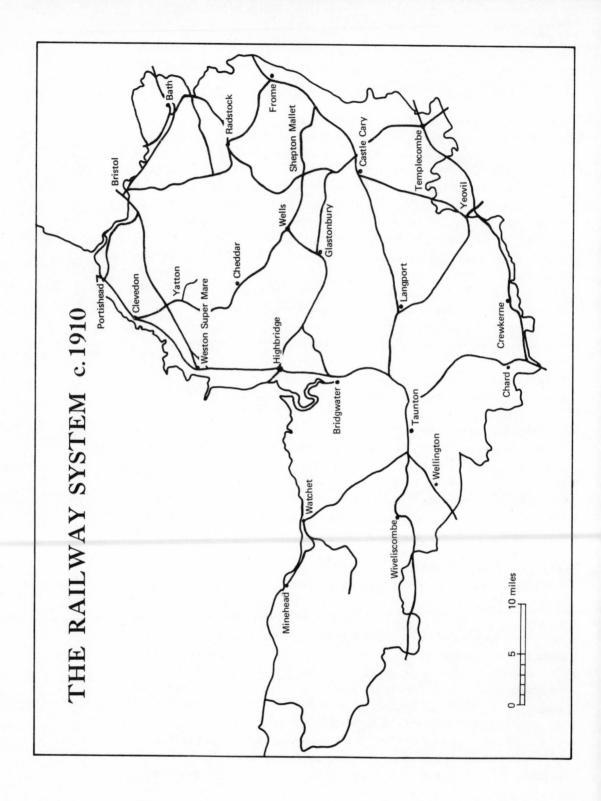

THE RAILWAY SYSTEM c.1910

Bath

Radstock

Frome

Shepton Mallet

Castle Cary

Templecombe

Bristol

Wells

Yeovil

Glastonbury

Portishead

Clevedon

Yatton

Cheddar

Langport

Weston Super Mare

Highbridge

Crewkerne

Bridgwater

Taunton

Chard

Watchet

Wellington

Wiveliscombe

Minehead

10 miles

5

0

43. Edward Berkeley Portman, 1st Viscount
Portman (1799-1888); Lord-Lieutenant of Somerset
1839-64. (*Somerset County Library*)

44. Henry Tuson of Northover, Ilchester, county clerk
of Somerset, about 1868. (*J. Stevens Cox*)

45. Transport of delight: a circus comes to Bath by railroad. (*Somerset Archaeological Society*)

46. A press of steamrollers: Sidney and Norman Buncombe of Highbridge with their engines, 1962. (*Somerset County Library*)

SOMERSET RELAXES:
47. Cricket at the County Ground, Taunton, in the mid 1960s; the crowds in the 1980s are fantastic.

(Somerset County Cricket Club)
48. Squibbing at Bridgwater Carnival, the largest in the county. *(Douglas Allen Photography)*

SOMERSET CRAFTSMEN
49. Bridgwater tile makers: Colthurs
Symonds and Co. Ltd., early 1960s.
(*Douglas Allen Photography*)

50. Oliver Stone of Bawdrip, blind
basket maker, *c.*1950. (*Douglas Allen
Photography*)

51. John Leach of Muchelney,
potter, 1983. (*R. J. Whittick*)

Yatton on the Bristol line to Cheddar, the romantic Cheddar Valley line. Yeovil, with four stations, Wells with three, and others with two, made rail travel in Somerset of the greatest value in the economic and social life of the county. Each station was a depot for agricultural and industrial products, and farms and businesses in all but the remote west were brought into communication with the rest of the commercial world.

Just as the farming landscape of open fields and undrained marsh had virtually disappeared, so, too, did the traditional cropping. Grain could be bought easily where the land would not produce it well, and the village baker by the early years of the 20th century was at the end of a chain which involved farmers in Canada and the United States and importers in Bridgwater and Bristol. Somerset grew more naturally the rich grass with which by nature it was blessed. By 1904, 71 per cent. of its 1,043,409 acres were grassland or orchards, supporting 478,447 sheep, 113,572 milking cows, and 129,869 other cattle. For centuries the farmers in the Bristol and Bath region had supplied produce to those two cities, and in the 1860s the proprietors of hotels and boarding houses in Weston super Mare were also in the market, buying up lambs at Congresbury spring fair to satisfy the appetites of their visitors. But only through the railway network was it practicable for a Liverpool purveyor, advertising in the *Weston Mercury* in 1867, to require weekly supplies of new potatoes, gooseberries and other early garden produce. Where once Somerset's wool had been in demand, now Somerset's butter and cheese, strawberries, sheepskins, and shoes were required.

The railways also revolutionised the social life of the county. After the County Council was established in 1889 its committee meetings were held as conveniently at Bridgwater and Highbridge as in Taunton and Wells, and members met as often as not in railway hotels as in public buildings. Communications were so good, it seems, that offices of the Council were to be found in Bath, Wells, Glastonbury, Frome, and Weston super Mare. And this mobility was soon being enjoyed by all. In 1872, when Francis Kilvert visited Taunton, he found members of an archaeological society touring the local churches in drays and 'two Antediluvian parsons in a gig, who seemed to have been thrown out and to be making a steeple chase towards Trull Church to fall in with the rest of the Archaeologists'. In 1880 the Rev. S. O. Baker of Muchelney, much more advanced in his notions, took 30 members of the Muchelney and Low Ham choirs on their annual treat, going by train from Langport to Weston junction, and thence by carriages to Burrington Combe. By the turn of the century the annual outing from Merriott was even more adventurous, those not content with the sands and shops of Weston taking a steamer trip across

'Clevedon', of the Weston, Clevedon and Portishead railway

97

Directory advertising, 1914

the Bristol Channel to Cardiff. Indeed, those steamers, plying along the coast from Weston to Lilstock, Watchet and Minehead, were an important attraction to the growing holiday market.

The railways had played a vital part in the creation of the resorts of Weston, Clevedon and Minehead. By the turn of the century they were creating a land market more familiar to more modern times. A proposal for a line from Minehead to Porlock was seriously canvassed so that the north coast of Exmoor might be opened for development, providing weekend cottages for Welsh businessmen. Prospective purchasers of these havens of peace had, however, to be guaranteed a return to their offices on Monday mornings, and the proposers of the scheme proved unable to control the tides at Watchet harbour on which all depended. Sites in the Quantocks for chalets and bungalows were offered for sale during the same period, and all along the coast of west Somerset apartments were offered to holidaymakers brought so near by the railway.

Castle Cary lock-up

The county was thus open to people from a wider world, a world glimpsed in every village in letters home from emigrants, in tales told by soldiers who had served with the county regiments in Egypt or India and by navigators on the canals and railways. And it came at that great 19th-century institution, the village school. There had, of course, been schools in the county for centuries: a grammar school at Wells before 1185, another at Taunton by 1286, and one at Bridgwater by 1298, all founded by churchmen; chantry schools like the one at Woolavington, where in the 1380s John Hody, son of a peasant, could learn enough to go to Oxford and become a rich man; foundations by laymen, such as the grammar school at Ilminster, founded in 1549, or its like at Martock, where Thomas Farnaby, an educationalist with an European reputation, began as master in 1605. By the mid 17th century there were small schools all over the county often kept, like the one at Williton, by a clergyman dispossessed of his living after the Civil War; and others run by Dissenters removed when the Church of England was restored. Bruton had seven schools in 1665, one taught by a Dissenter, and Shepton Mallet had five schools.

In the early 18th century Henry Grove's Dissenting Academy at Taunton was 'one of the most celebrated in all the West', and attracted the sons of prosperous families. A similar school at Watchet at the end of the century was, however, rejected by a prospective parent in favour of a rival at Bridgwater: 'I grant you the expences is more', he wrote, 'but I consider the [*sic*] larn as much in one week at Bwater as in two at Watchet'.

Free elementary schooling had been offered at East Harptree and High Ham in the late 16th century, and by the early 19th there were

Hannah More of Wrington

as many as 80 'blue coat' or charity schools in the county. Sunday schools for children who worked on weekdays appeared by the 1780s, and the energetic Hannah More established 11 of her schools in Mendip villages between 1789 and 1799. She was not aiming, as she often said when attacked by local landowners, to produce scholars, only to 'form the lower class to habits of industry and virtue'. Neither landowners nor many parents believed her.

By 1818 there were 109 endowed schools, 487 day schools, and 253 Sunday schools in the county. Many were very small and short-lived, often dame schools where an ignorant old woman earned a few pence teaching simple letters and numbers. Only a few of the old grammar schools survived to respectability, including one at Ilminster, where in the 1820s the master introduced talks on optics and astronomy, engaged a dancing master (whose class clashed with Latin and was therefore popular), and only failed to have gymnastics because of the exorbitant charges of the teacher. Young William Halliday assured his Mama in 1830 that he had not till then been 'folaged', but was sure that 'Mr. Allen has had many intentions to it'. Twenty-two years later he and his family were massacred at Cawnpore.

After 1870 a village school education of a reasonable standard was available to all. If few village children achieved the highest flights of learning, few could have been unaware of a wider world, where red seemed to encompass and dominate the globe. It was truly the end of an era when the Queen Empress died in 1901, an event to be marked at Barrington school, and doubtless in most others, when the mistress shared with her pupils 'a few facts', as she recorded in her log book, about the queen's last hours.

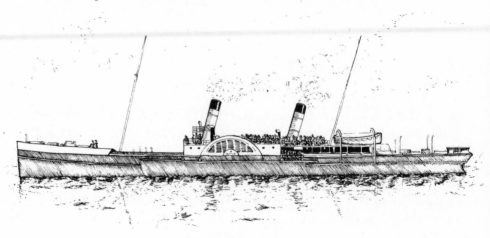

P.S. Brighton, 1878

XII The Twentieth Century

Chipstable and Raddington annual Bank Holiday fête and sports on 3 August 1914 was but one of a long tradition of public amusements in west Somerset whose origins could be traced back to the wrestling, cudgel-playing and horse-racing events at Maundown above Wiveliscombe at the turn of the 19th century. But instead of the handsome prizes and even more handsome wagers for the successful exertions of Charles Shetler, the cudgel champion of 1806, Chipstable sports were modest and gentlemanly. There were 16 healthy sports for very modest rewards, refreshments organised by the ladies of the parish, sideshows no more thrilling than a shooting gallery and the 'Electric Shock' administered by the rector, the whole enjoyed to the strains of the Bampton band. But on that very day war broke out; Chipstable, and every other village of its kind, was never to be the same again.

Burrow Mump

The First World War involved even the smallest and remotest community, and each war memorial is still eloquent of the huge loss of life. Exton, a parish of under 300 people, sent 44 men to war, and eight did not return; the tiny hamlet of Galmington lost seven men in a single year. Burrow Mump, rising above the Levels near Athelney, serves as a permanent memorial to 11,281 Somerset men who gave their lives.

For those too old or too young to fight the war made great if unrecognised demands. The County Archaeological Society abandoned its annual excursions, and one member lost his luggage when he found himself in charge of civilians leaving Germany in a hurry. The parish council at Compton Dundon called a meeting about the Prince of Wales's Fund in 1914. In 1915 they supported the parish Relief Committee in raising funds for Belgium, collected £11 11s. 6d. to be shared between the Serbian Relief Fund and the *Daily Express* Fund for providing tuck boxes for soldiers, and delivered recruitment cards to likely volunteers. At the end of 1917 they bought Scottish seed potatoes from the County Council. That was, as their clerk recorded their business, their official connection with the war, though as churchgoers they had no doubt prayed for victory according to the archbishops' direction in 1915 and had, perhaps, signed a petition organised by the *Morning Post* calling on God 'for the Deliverance of the British Nation from the Godless Menace and from the present distress and perplexity'.

*Arms of Somerset
County Council*

The young, too, took their share in the burden of the war. The children of Barrington school met a refugee Belgian priest in 1915, and in 1916 were knitting socks for the troops. They sang patriotic songs, flew flags and recited verses on Empire Day; they heard of the death of Lord Kitchener; and actually talked to an old pupil, Driver Tratt, who answered their questions about his work 'over in France'. They had the day off when the mistress saw her brother off as he returned to the Flanders Front; they knew the White family whose father was killed, and they played with the two boys who went to Taunton when their father returned to a military hospital in Swansea.

A Belgian refugee and several children of soldiers camped in the parish were admitted to Bishops Lydeard school in 1915, but the need for strict economy prevented the award of prizes from central funds. The children raised 10s. 3d. through a penny collection required by the Overseas Club for chocolate and tobacco for the troops, and in 1917 the girls had extra cookery lessons organised by the County Food Saving Association. The children raised 18s. 6d. for Christmas presents for Somerset soldiers in 1917, and in the same year collected 14½ cwt. of horse chestnuts in response to a government appeal. All this might have made a welcome change from lessons, but the children could have been in no doubt about the tragedy of war. Early in 1915 their headmaster volunteered for service and joined the Somerset Light Infantry; early in 1919 he died of pneumonia in Bombay.

Peace celebrations in July 1919 left the children of Barrington and Shepton Beauchamp too tired to attend school after two days of jollification. On a more serious note, the war taught the church people of Wilton that private pews and privilege had to go: 'that any one of the men whose names are . . . on the Roll of Honour (of those who were in uniform) should ever be asked to give place to any one of us', wrote the vicar in his parish magazine, 'would not be what we wish'.

The men who returned came back to a changing county. The creation of Somerset County Council in 1889 and the formation of parish councils or parish meetings from 1894 had brought local government into the hands of elected representatives for the first time. The rule of squire and parson was by no means immediately ended, and the first county aldermen and councillors included two Luttrells, a Hood, and a Horner, and five of the seven members of parliament for the county. But it also included men with industrial and commercial interests: a Clark from Street, a Fox from Wellington, a Bradford from Yeovil, and a Dening from Chard, representing shoes and cloth, transport and engineering.

The new council began with six officers and committees covering public works, police, contagious diseases of animals, and the lunatic

102

asylum. Education, welfare and planning were later added to its concerns by national legislation, and one of its members, the Rt. Hon. Henry Hobhouse (member 1889–1937, chairman 1904–24) was a leading figure of national importance in the development of local government. In 1934 the Council commissioned a planning survey of the county which suggested lines along which industry, agriculture and housing might develop in the future, involving improvements in the road system, so much more busy under the growing pressure from the motor car. The survey established the notion of landscape amenity which was proving of growing interest to visitors coming to the county in greater numbers on holiday. But holidays in the country were soon to be forgotten.

Development plans for a brave new world when the depression should end were shelved in the face of the second world crisis of the 20th century. Somerset was seen as a safe haven should hostilities break out and, in September 1939, 10,336 children arrived at Weston super Mare station from Bushey, Eltham, Limehouse, Poplar, and Kennington, half to be billeted on the town, half to be found homes in the neighbouring villages. Children from the London area, from Bristol and South Wales were distributed in their thousands among Somerset schools, usually having classes on a shift system.

The traditional harvest homes at Sandford, Mark, Churchill, and many another place were cancelled; so, too, were the North Somerset Yeomanry sports and gymkhana at Hutton. Cairns of stones and iron stakes were placed on beaches to slow down an invader, road signs were taken away, trees were felled in level fields, committees for home defence were set up in every village, and units of the Home Guard took over every available hall. Three of the familiar vessels of the White Funnel fleet at Weston went down at Dunkirk; the first bombs fell outside Taunton in June 1940, and every child at school, equipped with gas mask, was instructed in proper action in the event of an air raid. At Burnham they were to shelter under the Esplanade; at Withycombe to seek refuge in the rectory garden; at South Petherton to march to the cricket field and lie under a hedge with the teachers; at Shapwick to sit under desks and sing. The children at Pill, near Bristol, were either to go home or to the church; the church was later bombed.

In war the countryside changed: by night all was dark; by day farmers were ploughing grassland, digging for victory. Forty-eight thousand acres were added to the arable total before war broke out, and 13,000 more people found jobs on the land. By 1942 the arable acreage was doubled as less and less food could be imported. The last great drainage enterprise on the Levels, the Huntspill river, was cunningly achieved at the same time, since it provided essential water

The Rt. Hon. Henry Hobhouse

103

Pillbox

for the Royal Ordnance factory at Puriton. Thirteen airfields in the county, which served as bases for allied forces preparing the long build-up to the D-Day landings in France, have largely disappeared, but the Admiralty at Bath, and the American 67th General Hospital at Taunton, now Musgrove Park, are reminders of the military presence in the county, and country houses and their parks still bear scars from their use as training camps and munition dumps. Fields still have traces of searchlight batteries, barrage balloon bases, storage depots, and the tell-tale pillboxes which formed possible lines of defence across the county. In the towns there are still faint traces of paint on signs which once pointed to an A.R.P. post or recruiting office. The sacrifice and the effort of Somerset people can never be accurately assessed, but the bombing suffered at Bath in 1942 and the vast sum of nearly £8 million raised in Taunton alone in the various savings campaigns affected the lives of countless people.

Post-war Somerset, like post-war Britain, is a story of widening government involvement at national and local level against a background of austerity, recovery, boom and crisis. Closure of railways and coal mines affected employees, consumers, and the countryside. The importance of that countryside has figured prominently in development plans in the county, though the balance between various interests still causes controversy. The creation of Exmoor National Park in 1954 and the declaration of the Quantocks as an Area of Outstanding Natural Beauty in 1957 were the beginning of a process whereby areas of the county have been preserved in various ways. Woods, heathland and marsh have been set aside because of their interest to naturalists, and a large area of West Sedgemoor was in 1983 the latest subject of concern.

The notable growth of population in the north of the county had been recognised in the 1930s and by the 1960s Bristol was clearly the economic focus of a wide area of Somerset. Local government reorganisation, which came into effect on 1 April 1974, transferred a large and populous area north of the Mendip scarp to a new county of Avon, creating a boundary which in some cases ran arbitrarily through ancient parishes. The new creation was not popular among many people on both sides of the boundary, and returning to Somerset continues to be the aim of some, prompted both by a larger rates burden and by a deep loyalty to a county which seems to be offended by an action against a thousand years of history.

Historic Somerset still continues, whatever the governing veneer. For a thousand years and more the people living between the Bristol Avon and the Mendips were Somerset folk, as well as those living beyond Mendip. Theirs was a heritage which was affected neither by

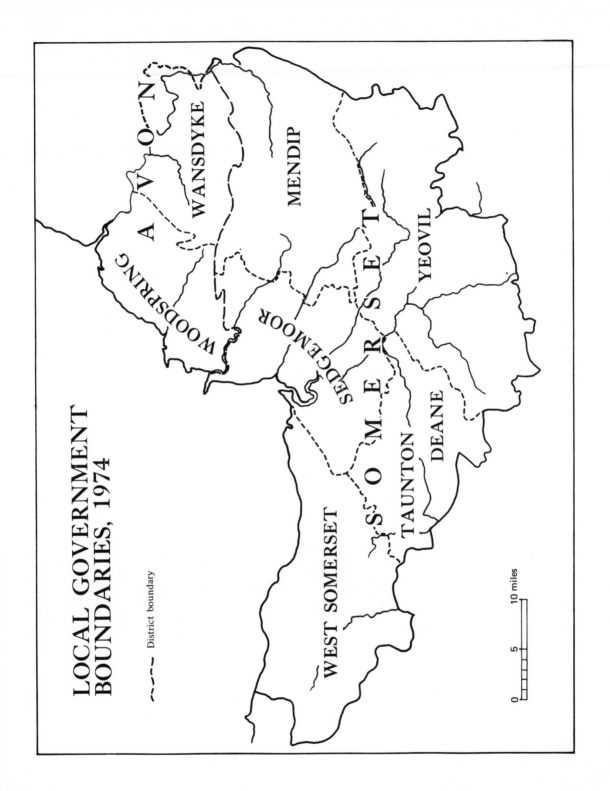

LOCAL GOVERNMENT
BOUNDARIES, 1974

----- District boundary

A V O N

WANSDYKE

MENDIP

WOODSPRING

SEDGEMOOR

S O M E R S E T

YEOVIL

WEST SOMERSET

TAUNTON
DEANE

0   5   10 miles

105

the creation of Somerset County Council in 1889, nor by that of Avon in 1974. That heritage is a story of gentle change, not of a stagnant past. The long-established manufacture of cloth throughout the county has given place in modern times to shoes, cellophane, and aircraft; its small-scale production of teazel or rope to micro-manipulators whose precision measurements have made them essential in cancer research and in the analysis of moon rocks at the N.A.S.A. space centre in the U.S.A. The rich grassland which became a war-time airfield at Yeovilton in 1919 was the home base of men who saw service in the Falklands in 1982, and the Fleet Air Arm museum there displays not only Concorde 002, but also trophies from the South Atlantic. Cheddar cheese has recently received an accolade from Continental experts which Somerset folk have given it for generations, and soft cheeses are coming from dairies at Cannington and near Crewkerne, a proper challenge to makers across the Channel from the county which has such a long tradition of milk products. Farming is still Somerset's major industry, but tourism is not far behind. The county's tradition, so clear to see in the buildings of its towns and villages, so charming to hear from Somerset people, so exciting to explore in its countryside, is the key to its attraction to increasing numbers of people who visit it every year.

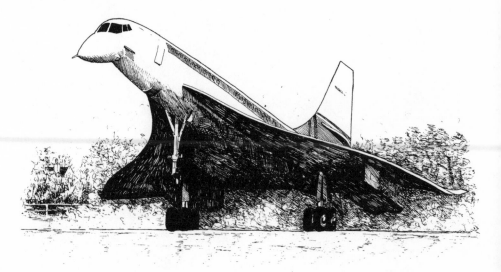

Concorde 002

APPENDIX ONE

Bishops of the Diocese

Bishops of Wells

909	Athelm	997	Aelfwine
923	Wulfhelm	999	Lifing or Ethelstan
926	Aelfheah	1013	Aethelwine
938	Wulfhelm	1023-4	Brithwy or Merehwit
956	Brithelm	1033	Duduc
974	Cyneweard	1061	Giso
975	Sigegar		

Bishop Giso

Bishops of Bath

1088	John de Villula (John of Tours)	1136	Robert of Lewes
1123	Godfrey	1174	Reginald FitzJocelin

Bishops of Bath and Glastonbury

1192	Savaric FitzGeldewin	1206	Jocelin of Wells (Jocelin Trotman)

Bishops of Bath and Wells

1244	Roger	1424	John Stafford
1248	William Button I	1443	Thomas Beckington
1264	Walter Giffard	1465	Robert Stillington
1267	William Button II	1492	Richard Fox
1275	Robert Burnell	1495	Oliver King
1293	William of March	1504	Hadrian de Castello
1302	Walter Haselshaw	1518	Thomas Wolsey
1309	John Droxford	1523	John Clerk
1329	Ralph of Shrewsbury	1541	William Knight
1363	John Barnet	1548	William Barlow
1366	John Harewell	1554	Gilbert Bourne
1386	Walter Skirlaw	1560	Gilbert Berkeley
1388	Ralph Erghum	1584	Thomas Godwin
1401	Henry Bowet	1593	John Still
1407	Nicholas Bubwith	1608	James Montague

1616	Arthur Lake	1802	Richard Beadon
1626	William Laud	1824	George Henry Law
1628	Leonard Mawe	1845	Richard Bagot
1629	Walter Curll	1854	Robert John Eden, Baron Auckland
1632	William Piers		
1670	Robert Creighton	1869	Lord Arthur Charles Hervey
1672	Peter Mews	1894	George Wyndham Kennion
1684	Thomas Ken	1921	St John Basil Wynne Willson
1691	Richard Kidder	1937	Francis Underhill
1703	George Hooper	1943	John William Charles Wand
1727	John Wynne	1946	Harold William Bradfield
1743	Edward Willes	1960	Edward Barry Henderson
1774	Charles Moss	1975	John Monier Bickersteth

APPENDIX TWO

Lord-Lieutenants of Somerset

1559, 1569	William Herbert, 1st Earl of Pembroke, K.G., P.C.
by 1585–1601	Henry Herbert, 2nd Earl of Pembroke, K.G., K.B.
1601–1621	Edward Seymour, 1st Earl of Hertford, K.B.
1621–1630	William Herbert, 3rd Earl of Pembroke, K.G.
1630–1642	Philip Herbert, 4th Earl of Pembroke, K.G., K.B.
1642	William Seymour, 1st Marquess of Hertford, K.G., K.B., P.C.
1642	William Russell, 5th Earl of Bedford, K.B.
1643	Philip Herbert, 4th Earl of Pembroke, K.G., K.B.
1660	William Seymour, 1st Marquess of Hertford and 2nd Duke of Somerset, K.G., K.B., P.C.
1660–1672	James Butler, 1st Marquess and 1st Duke of Ormond, K.G., P.C.
1672–1675	John Seymour, 4th Duke of Somerset
1675–1683	Heneage Finch, 3rd Earl of Winchilsea
1683–1687	Charles Seymour, 6th Duke of Somerset, K.G.
1687–1688	Henry Waldegrave, 1st Baron Waldegrave
1688	Ralph Stawell, 1st Baron Stawell
1689–1690	Maurice Berkeley, 3rd Viscount Fitzhardinge
1691–1714	James Butler, 2nd Duke of Ormond, K.G., P.C.
1714–1715	Charles Boyle, 4th Earl of Orrery, K.T., P.C.
1715–1720	George Dodington, P.C.
1720–1744	George Bubb Dodington, P.C.
1744–1764	John Poulett, 2nd Earl Poulett
1764–1774	Percy Wyndham O'Brien, 1st Earl of Thomond, P.C.
1774–1792	Frederick North, Lord North, 2nd Earl of Guilford, K.G.
1792–1819	John Poulett, 4th Earl Poulett, K.T.
1819–1837	Thomas Thynne, 2nd Marquess of Bath, K.G.
1837–1839	Henry Stephen Fox-Strangways, 3rd Earl of Ilchester, P.C.
1839–1864	Edward Berkeley Portman, 1st Baron Portman
1864–1904	Richard Edward St Lawrence Boyle, 9th Earl of Cork, K.P., P.C.

Frederick, Lord North

Lord-Lieutenants of Somerset—*continued*

1904–1946   Thomas Henry Thynne, 5th Marquess of Bath, K.G., P.C.
1946–1949   James Fownes Somerville, G.C.B., G.B.E.
1949–1967   William George Hervey Jolliffe, 4th Baron Hylton
1967–1978   Cecil Townley Mitford-Slade
1978–   Geoffrey Walter Fownes Luttrell

*Arms of
John Clevedon*

APPENDIX THREE

Sheriffs of Somerset

The names of only a few sheriffs of Somerset have been found before 1154. Godwine is named in 1061, and Tovid or Tofig was sheriff when the Normans invaded, and was still in office in 1068. William de Mohun was the first of the Norman sheriffs, in office by 1083, and when Domesday Book was compiled in 1086. Perhaps he remained sheriff until his death *c.* 1090. Aiulph, the royal chamberlain, already sheriff of Dorset, was also sheriff of Somerset by 1091 and until well into the reign of Henry I; Warin followed him in Dorset and before 1123 in Somerset, and continued until *c.* 1130. Thereafter, with a few exceptions, the sheriffs held office for Somerset and Dorset jointly until 1567.

1155	Richard de Monte Alto	1212	Richard de Marisco, clerk
1155	Richard de Raddona	1214	William de Harcourt
1157	Warner de Lisoriis	1215	Ralph de Bray
1158	Richard de Raddona	1216	Peter de Maulay
1160	Warner de Lisoriis	1217	William Longespee, earl of Salisbury (Somerset only)
1162	Robert de Beauchamp		
1163	Gerbert de Percy	1217	Peter de Maulay
1167	Robert Pucherel	1221	Roger de la Forde
1169	Alfred of Lincoln	1223	John Russell (Somerset only)
1175	Robert de Beauchamp	1223	Jocelin, Bishop of Bath and Wells (Somerset only)
1182	William de Bendeng		
1184	Robert Fitzpain	1226	William FitzHenry
1188	Hugh Bardolf	1228	Thomas de Cirencester
1189	John, count of Mortain	1232	Peter de Rievaux
1194	William, earl of Salisbury	1232	Thomas de Cirencester
1194	William de Cahaignes	1233	Henry FitzNicholas
1197	Peter de Scudamore	1234	Thomas de Cirencester
1199	Robert Belet	1237	Richard de Langford
1200	Hubert de Burgh	1238	Herbert FitzMatthew
1204	William de Montacute	1239	Jordan Oliver
	Osbert de Stoke	1240	Hugh de Vivonia
1207	William Brewer	1242	Joel de Valletort
1209	William Malet	1249	Godfrey de Scudamore

1249	Bartholomew Petch		1338	Walter Rodney
1250	Henry de Erleigh		1340	John Durburgh
1251	Elias de Rabayn		1340	Walter Rodney
1254	John de Aller		1340	John Durburgh
1254	Stephen de Ashton		1341	Hugh Tyrel
1257	Walter de Burges		1343	Edward Stradling
1258	William Everard		1343	Thomas Cary
1259	Philip de Cerne		1353	John Palton
1261	Philip Basset		1355	John St Loe
1263	Henry, son of Richard, earl of Cornwall		1356	Richard Turbervill
			1358	Robert Martyn
1264	William de Staunton		1359	John de Raleigh
1265	Ralph Russell		1360	Nicholas St Maur
1266	Philip Basset		1360	Edmund de Clevedon
1267	Andrew Wake		1361	Theobald Gorges
1269	Thomas de St Vigor		1361	Thomas de Bridport
1273	John de St Valery		1362	John de la Hale
1274	Richard de Coleshill		1364	John de Langlonde
1278	John de Cormailles		1368	Edmund Cheyney
1283	John de St Loe		1370	William Winterbourne
1285	Queen Eleanor		1371	Roger Manningford
1289	Richard de Burghunte		1372	John Hamelyn, knight
1291	Walter de Luveny		1373	Hugh Durburgh, knight
1293	Walter de Gloucester		1374	William Latimer
1298	Nicholas de Cheyney		1375	Edmund FitzHerbert, knight
1299	John Gerberge		1376	Hugh Durburgh, knight
1301	John de la Lee		1377	John de la Mare, knight
1302	John Gerberge		1378	William Cogan, knight
1304	Matthew Furneaux		1379	John Burghersh, knight
1305	John de Montacute		1380	Theobald Gorges
1306	Nicholas de Langlonde		1380	William Latimer
1307	Nicholas Cheyney		1381	William Bonville, knight
1308	Walter Scudamore		1382	Edmund FitzHerbert, knight
1309	Richard Chesilden		1383	John Strecche, knight
1311	Walter Scudamore		1384	John Burghersh, knight
1313	John Chideock		1385	John Copleston
1314	John de Erleigh		1386	Humphrey Stafford, knight
1315	Matthew Furneaux		1387	John Rodney, knight
1316	John de Kyngeston		1388	John Moigne, knight
1318	Nicholas Cheyney		1389	Thomas Brooke, knight
1320	Thomas de Marlberge		1390	John Berkeley, knight
1325	John de Erleigh		1391	Humphrey Stafford, knight
1326	Thomas de Marlberge		1392	John Bache
1327	William de Whitefield		1393	Theobald Wykeham
1330	Hugh de Langlonde		1394	John Berkeley, knight
1332	John de Wraxhall		1395	John Moigne, knight
1333	Hildebrand of London		1396	John Rodney, knight
1335	Walter Rodney		1397	Thomas Arthur, knight
1336	Hildebrand of London		1397	Thomas Daccombe, knight

Arms of Walter Rodney

110

1399	Thomas Arthur, knight	1445	John Norris
1400	Richard Boyton	1446	William Carent
1401	John Luttrell, knight	1447	John Chideock, knight
1402	John Frome	1448	Edward Hull, knight
1403	William Wroth	1449	John Austell
1404	Thomas Pomeroy, knight	1450	William Carent
1405	Humphrey Stafford, knight	1451	Thomas Thame
1405	Richard Boyton	1452	Richard Warre
1406	Walter Rodney, knight	1453	Nicholas Latimer
1407	John Horsey	1454	John Cheyney
1408	Robert Hill	1455	John Willoughby
1408	Matthew Coker	1456	Nicholas St Loe
1409	Richard Boyton	1457	Robert Warre
1410	Humphrey Stafford, knight	1458	John St Barbe
1411	John Horsey	1459	John Carent
1412	Robert Hill	1460	Humphrey Stafford
1413	Walter Hungerford, knight	1461	Thomas Herbert
1414	John Warre	1463	William Browning
1415	Humphrey Stafford, knight, of Hook	1464	Christopher Worseley
		1465	John Sydenham
1416	Richard Boyton	1466	George Darell
1417	Matthew Coker	1467	Robert Stawell
1418	John Florey	1468	Reginald Stourton, knight
1419	Robert Hill	1469	Christopher Worseley
1420	John Newburgh	1470	Nicholas Latimer, knight
1422	Robert Hill	1471	John Cheverell
1422	Robert Coker	1472	John Biconyll
1423	Richard Stafford, knight	1473	Robert Palmer
1424	Edward Stradling, knight	1474	Giles Daubeney
1426	Giles Daubeney, knight	1475	William Collingbourne
1426	William Finderne	1476	Thomas Norton
1427	William Carent	1477	William Berkeley
1428	John Stourton, knight	1478	William Say
1430	John Warre	1479	Edward Hartgill
1430	John Paulet	1480	Giles Daubeney
1431	John Stourton	1481	Richard Morton
1432	John St Loe	1482	Nicholas Crowmer
1433	John Seymour	1483	Edward Redmayne
1434	William Carent	1484	Thomas Fulford, knight
1435	Thomas Thame	1485	Amias Poulett
1436	John St Loe	1486	John Turbervill
1437	William Stafford	1487	James Daubeney
1438	Edward Hull	1488	Hugh Luttrell, knight
1439	Walter Rodney	1489	William Martin
1440	William Carent	1490	Henry Burnell
1441	William Stafford	1491	Amias Poulett, knight
1442	John St Loe	1492	Walter Enderby
1443	Edward Hull, knight	1493	Edmund Carew, knight
1444	Robert Cappes	1494	Sampson Norton, knight

Arms of John Sydenham

Nettlecombe chalice,
1479

1495	Edmund Gorges, knight
1496	Roger Newburgh
1497	Richard Pudsey, knight
1498	Nicholas Wadham
1499	Amias Poulett, knight
1500	William Martin
1501	John Trevelyan, knight
1502	Edward Wadham
1503	Henry Uvedale
1504	John Horsey
1505	John Sydenham
1506	John Carew, knight
1507	John Williams, knight
1508	John Bevyn
1508	Richard Weston
1509	Thomas Trenchard, knight
1510	John Speke, knight
1511	Walter Rodney
1512	Giles Strangways
1513	William Compton, knight
1514	Edward Gorges
1515	John Seymour, knight
1516	Thomas de la Lynd, knight
1517	Giles Strangways
1518	Edward Hungerford, knight
1519	John Bourchier
1520	William Wadham
1522	John Rogers
1522	William Carent
1523	Thomas Trenchard, knight
1524	Giles Strangways, knight
1526	George Speke
1526	John Seymour, knight
1527	John Russell, knight
1528	Andrew Luttrell
1529	Edward Gorges, knight
1530	Thomas Arundell
1531	Edward Seymour, knight
1532	Thomas More, knight
1533	Giles Strangways, knight
1534	Nicholas Wadham, knight
1535	Francis Dawtrey
1536	Hugh Poulett, knight
1537	John Horsey, knight
1538	Henry Long, knight
1539	Thomas Speke, knight
1540	Thomas Arundell, knight
1541	Giles Strangways, knight
1542	Hugh Poulett, knight
1543	John Poulett
1544	John Horsey, knight
1545	Nicholas FitzJames
1546	John Sydenham
1547	Hugh Poulett, knight
1548	John Thynne, knight
1549	Thomas Speke, knight
1550	George de la Lynd
1551	John St Loe, knight
1552	John Rogers, knight
1553	John Tregonwell, knight
1554	John Sydenham, knight
1555	Henry Ashley, knight
1556	John Wadham
1557	Humphrey Colles
1558	John Horsey, knight
1559	Thomas Dyer, knight
1560	James FitzJames, knight
1561	John Wyndham, knight
1562	George Speke, knight
1563	John Horner
1564	Henry Ashley, knight
1565	Henry Uvedale
1566	Thomas Morton
1567	Maurice Berkeley, knight
1568	George Norton, knight
1569	Henry Portman
1571	John Sydenham, of Leigh
1571	George Rogers
1572	John Horner
1573	John Sydenham, of Brympton
1574	John Stawell, knight
1575	Christopher Kenn
1576	Thomas Malet
1577	George Sydenham
1578	John Colles
1579	John Brett
1580	Maurice Rodney
1581	Henry Newton
1582	John Buller
1583	Arthur Hopton
1584	Gabriel Hawley
1585	Nicholas Wadham
1586	John Clifton, knight
1587	Henry Berkeley, knight
1588	Edward St Barbe
1589	Samuel Norton
1590	Hugh Portman

1591	John Harrington	1638	William Every
1592	George Speke	1639	Thomas Wroth, knight
1593	George Luttrell	1640	John Hippisley
1594	Henry Walrond	1641	Martin Sanford
1595	John Fraunceys	1642	Edmund Wyndham
1596	John Stawell, knight	1642	Thomas Brydges
1597	John Colles	1644	John Horner, knight
1598	John Jennings	1646	Richard Cole
1599	George Rodney	1647	John Preston
1600	Hugh Portman, knight	1648	John Buckland
1601	John Malet	1649	Henry Bonner
1602	John Mayo	1650	Alexander Pym
1603	Edward Rogers	1651	Edward Ceely
1604	John Wyndham, knight	1652	George Luttrell
1606	Thomas Horner	1653	William Cole
1606	John Portman	1654	Robert Hunt
1607	Edward Hext, knight	1656	William Hillyard
1608	Edward Gorges, knight	1659	William Lacey
1609	George Luttrell	1660	William Helyar
1610	Francis Baber	1661	George Speke
1611	John Rodney, knight	1662	John Warre, knight
1612	Hugh Smyth, knight	1663	George Newton, knight
1612	Robert Henley	1664	George Trevelyan, knight
1613	Nathaniel Still	1665	Hugh Smyth, bart.
1614	John Horner, knight	1666	George Stawell
1615	Bartholomew Michell, knight	1667	George Horner, knight
1616	John Colles	1668	Henry Rogers
1616	John Poulett	1669	Roger Bourne
1617	Robert Hopton	1670	Thomas Gore, knight
1618	Theodore Newton, knight	1671	William Strode
1619	John Trevelyan	1672	Francis Rolle, knight
1620	Henry Henley	1673	John Carew
1621	Marmaduke Jennings	1674	Halswell Tynte, bart.
1622	Edward Popham	1675	John Prowse
1623	William Fraunceys	1676	Ralph Stawell
1624	Thomas Wyndham	1676	Richard Lansdowne
1625	Robert Phelips, knight	1677	Gregory Heekmore, knight
1626	John Symes	1678	John Carew
1627	John Latch	1679	William Wyndham, bart.
1628	John Stawell, knight	1680	Maurice Berkeley, bart.
1629	Thomas Thynne, knight	1681	George Horner
1630	Francis Dodington, knight	1681	Thomas Warre
1631	Thomas Luttrell	1682	John Pigott
1632	William Walrond	1683	Henry Bull
1633	John Carew, knight	1684	Edward Hobbs
1634	Henry Hodges	1685	Edward Baber
1636	John Malet, knight	1686	James Prowse
1636	William Bassett	1687	Edward Strode
1637	William Portman, bart.	1688	John Smyth, bart.

Arms of
Sir William Wyndham

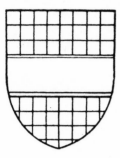

*Arms of Sir
Thomas Dyke Acland*

1689	Richard Morgan	1733	William Provis
1689	John Smyth, bart.	1734	Thomas Welman
1690	William Whitchurch	1734	John Brickdale
1691	William Lacey	1734	Joseph Langton
1692	Warwick Bampfield	1735	Orlando Johnson
1693	Robert Siderfin	1737	John Periam
1694	John Champneys	1738	James Chaffey Cowper
1695	Thomas Langton	1738	John Smith
1696	Thomas Dyke	1739	John Brickdale
1697	Joseph Langton	1740	John Freke Brickdale
1697	Henry Mompesson	1740	John Provis
1698	Smart Goodenough	1741	William Madox
1699	Francis Holles Newman	1741	Edward Hallett
1700	William Helyar	1741	William Pynsent, bart.
1702	Samuel Rodbard	1742	John Smith
1702	John Mogg	1743	William Sanford
1703	Samuel Pitt	1744	Edward Clarke
1704	John Trevelyan, bart.	1745	Francis Newman
1705	Thomas Warre	1746	John Halliday
1706	William Fraunceis	1747	Thomas Coles
1707	Robert Smith	1748	James Jeanes
1708	Thomas Wroth, bart.	1749	Matthew Spencer
1709	Isaac Welman	1750	Henry William Portman
1710	William Blackford	1751	Thomas Dyke Acland, bart.
1711	Thomas Horner	1752	John Harding
1712	Harry Brydges	1753	John Macie
1713	William Strode	1754	Henry Fownes Luttrell
1714	John Trevillian	1755	Roger Lyde
1715	Henry Walters	1756	James Perry
1716	Joseph Brown	1757	John Collins
1717	Thomas Archer	1758	Philip Stephens
1718	Robert Everard	1759	Henry Powell
1720	Jepp Clarke	1760	William Yea, bart.
1721	William Applin	1761	John Adams
1721	Henry Strode	1762	Thomas Gunston
1722	Richard Comes	1763	Samuel Dodington
1723	Walter Robinson	1764	William Helyar
1724	Christopher Baker	1765	Paris Taylor
1724	John Gatchell	1766	James Tooker
1724	Andrew Moore	1767	William Provis
1726	David Yea	1768	John Helliar
1726	Edward Dyke	1769	William Rodbard
1726	Edward Dyke, the younger	1770	Nathaniel Webb
1727	Richard Champneys	1771	Thomas Coward
1728	Gregory Gardiner	1772	Henry Rodbard
1729	John Pigott	1773	John Hugh Smyth
1730	William Fraunceis	1774	John Old Goodford
1731	John Proctor	1775	Thomas Champneys, bart.
1732	John Smyth, bart	1776	Thomas Wilkins Morgan

Year	Name	Year	Name
1777	John Trevelyan, bart.	1824	Edward Jefferies Esdaile
1778	Thomas Horner	1825	John Quantock
1779	Samuel Baker	1826	William Helyar
1780	Edward Elton	1827	Henry Powell Collins
1781	John Ford	1828	John Hugh Smyth Pigott
1782	James Ireland	1829	Alexander Hood, bart.
1783	Peter Sherston	1830	James Adam Gordon
1784	Andrew Guy	1831	Thomas Shewell Bailward
1785	Richard Crosse	1832	Henry Strachey, bart
1786	James Stephens	1833	George Henry Carew
1787	Nathaniel Dalton	1834	Francis Popham
1788	John Lethbridge	1835	William Manning Dodington
1789	Henry Hippisley Coxe	1836	James Bennett
1790	John Stephenson	1837	Alexander Adair
1791	Abraham Elton	1838	Robert Phippen
1792	Thomas Samuel Jolliffe	1839	William Coles Medlycott, bart.
1793	Samuel Bailward	1840	John Jarrett
1794	Charles Knatchbull	1841	William Francis Knatchbull
1795	Edward Lyne	1842	Robert Charles Tudway
1796	John Tyndale Warre	1843	Philip Pleydell-Bouverie
1797	Samuel Day	1844	John Fownes Luttrell
1798	Samuel Rodbard	1845	John Lee Lee
1799	James Bennett	1846	Richard Meade-King
1800	Thomas Swymmer Champneys	1847	John Matthew Quantock
1801	John Band	1848	Edward Ayshford Sanford
1802	Benjamin Greenhill	1849	George Wynter Blathwayt
1803	Hugh Smyth, bart.	1850	Langley St Albyn
1804	John Rogers	1851	Thomas Tutton Knyfton
1805	John Perring	1852	Montague Gore
1806	Clifton Wheate	1853	Francis Henry Dickinson
1807	John Hawkins, bart.	1854	James Curtis Somerville
1808	Charles Kemeys-Tynte	1855	George Barons Northcote
1809	John Nurton	1856	John Hippisley
1810	Thomas Strangways Horner	1857	Arthur Hallam Elton, bart.
1811	John Leigh	1858	Alexander Acland-Hood, bart.
1812	William Vaughan	1859	Edward Berkeley Napier
1813	Peregrine Palmer Acland	1860	Robert James Elton
1814	George Edward Allen	1861	Francis Wheat Newton
1815	John Phelips	1862	Ralph Neville-Grenville
1816	John Goodford	1863	George Treweeke Scobell
1817	Philip John Miles	1864	Edward Strachey, bart.
1818	John Everard	1865	John Hugh Greville Smyth, bart.
1819	William Speke		
1820	Gerard Martin Berkeley Napier	1866	George Bullock
1820	Charles Warwick Bamfylde, bart.	1867	Richard Thomas Combe
		1868	Inigo William Jones
1821	William Hanning	1869	William Blake
1822	Vincent Stuckey	1870	Robert Guy Evered
1823	John Frederick Pinney	1871	Henry Cornish Henley

Arms of
Sir John Trevelyan

115

*Arms of
Robert Hill*

1872	Mordaunt Fenwick Bisset
1873	Richard King Meade-King
1874	George Fownes Luttrell
1875	Henry Georges Moysey
1876	Henry Duncan Skrine
1877	William Pinney
1878	Philip Pleydell-Bouverie
1879	Edward Charles Chetham-Strode
1880	Edward James Stanley
1881	Henry Acland Fownes Luttrell
1882	Thomas Palfrey Broadmead
1883	Vincent Stuckey
1885	Charles Jefferys Watson Allen
1885	John Francis Fortescue Horner
1886	Alexander William Adair
1887	Thomas Marriott-Dodington
1888	Anthony Gibbs
1889	Charles Edward Jeffries Esdaile
1890	Edward Talbot Day Foxcroft
1891	William Wildman Kettlewell
1892	William Barrett
1893	Henry Ernst
1894	William Speke
1895	Edmund Harry Elton, bart.
1896	Robert Pooll Henry Batten-Pooll
1897	Henry Martin Gibbs
1898	Edward William Berkeley Portman
1899	William Long
1900	Robert Neville-Grenville
1901	William Robert Phelips
1902	Edwin Brooke Cely-Trevilian
1903	Frederick Spencer
1904	Henry Hales Pleydell-Bouverie
1905	William Henry Wills, bart.
1906	Francis James Fry
1907	Richard John Baynton Hippisley
1908	Edward Charles Sanford
1909	Arthur Fownes Luttrell
1910	Henry Herbert Wills
1911	Charles Edward Heley Chadwyck-Healey, knight
1912	William Bucknell Broadmead
1913	Henry William Paget Hoskins
1914	Joseph Cooke Hurle
1915	Gerard Berkeley Napier
1916	Francis Henry Cheetham
1917	Gerard Stuart Lysaght
1918	Henry Thomas Daniel
1918	Arthur Vaughan Hanning Vaughan-Lee
1920	Henry Matthew Ridley
1921	Arthur Capel
1922	Roger Marriott Dodington
1923	Denis Fortescue Boles, bart.
1924	Arthur Campbell Duckworth
1925	Maurice Fearing Cely-Trevilian
1926	Frank Beauchamp, bart.
1927	Walter Hanning Speke
1928	William Peake Mason, bart
1929	Harold Hamilton Broadmead
1930	Huntley Gordon Spencer
1931	William Oliver Evelyn Meade-King, knight
1932	Reginald Arthur Hobhouse
1933	William Hartley Maud
1934	Matthew Nathan, P.C.,G.C.M.G.
1935	Geoffrey Fownes Luttrell
1936	William Otto Gibbs
1937	James Archibald Garton
1938	Archibald Lawrence Langman, bart.
1939	Frederick Henry Berryman, knight
1940	Arthur Hamilton Yatman
1941	Edward Philip Thursfield
1942	Charles Edward Burnell
1943	Arthur Westall Vivian-Neal
1944	Frederick Willoughby Hancock
1945	Edmund Fletcher Rees-Mogg
1946	Walter Stewart Batten-Pooll
1946	Walter Douglas Melville Wills
1947	Edmund Page
1948	Hubert Stanley Radcliffe
1949	Henry Cave Daniel
1950	Henry William Whitby Hoskins
1951	Robert John Sinclair, knight
1952	Arthur John Capel
1953	Wilfrid Leighton
1954	Walter Frank Quantock Shuldham
1955	Roger Evans
1956	John Kenric La Touche Mardon

Sheriffs of Somerset—*continued*

1957	John Goodenough Newton	1969	William Quincey Roberts
1958	Wilfrid Anson, knight	1970	John Anthony Clark
1959	Nicholas Brabazon Clive-Ponsonby-Fane	1971	Henry William Furse Hoskins
		1972	Colin John Clifford Trotter
1960	Geoffrey Walter Fownes Lut-trell	1973	Gerald Worthington Hignett
		1974	David Cuthbert Tudway Quil-ter
1961	Richard Edwin Fearing Cely-Trevilian	1975	Matthew Henry Waley-Cohen
1962	Gilbert Sandford Poole	1976	John Stephen Lloyd
1963	Cecil Townley Mitford-Slade	1977	Patrick Henry Daniel
1964	Richard Hill	1978	William Rees-Mogg
1965	John Cotesworth Slessor, G.C.B.	1979	William Kenneth Bingham Crawford
1966	Edward St Lo Malet, bart.	1980	John Lindley
1967	Ian Duff Lyle, knight	1981	Arthur John Greswell
1968	John Vernon Wills, bart.	1982	Peter Gerald Hanning Speke
1969	Hugh Webb Faulkner	1983	Count Charles John de Salis

APPENDIX FOUR

Chairmen of Somerset County Council

1889–1900	The Rt. Hon. Sir Richard Paget, bart, M.P.
1900–1904	A. J. Goodford
1904–1924	The Rt. Hon. Henry Hobhouse, M.P.
1924–1927	J. Cooke Hurle
1927–1932	Sir Frederick Berryman
1932–1937	Captain the Hon. T. H. Watson
1937–1940	The Rt. Hon. the Lord Bayford, D.L.
1940–1947	Sir Arthur Hobhouse
1947–1952	Colonel E. R. Clayton, C.M.G., D.S.O., D.L.
1952–1955	Major H. W. W. Hoskyns, T.D., D.L.
1955–1956	F. H. F. Calway, D.L.
1956–1959	A. Whittaker, C.S.I., C.I.E.
1959–1964	Brigadier E. H. C. Frith, C.B.E., D.L.
1964–1969	Lieutenant-Colonel G. C. G. Grey, O.B.E.
1969–1974	G. C. Wyndham, D.L.

(Under the Local Government Act 1972)

1973–1974	Dr. D. C. Green
1974–1978	W. M. F. Knowles, O.B.E.
1978–1983	Air Vice-Marshall H. G. Leonard-Williams, C.B., C.B.E., D.L.
1983–	W. R. Meadows

Rebus of Bishop Oliver King, Bath abbey

SOURCES FOR FURTHER STUDY

General

In 1791 the Revd. John Collinson published his *History of Somerset* (new edition, including Index and supplement, Alan Sutton 1983) which included a history of every parish in the county, based in part on sources now lost. Since 1849 the Somerset Archaeological and Natural History Society has been issuing annual volumes of *Proceedings*, which are a fine source of wide-ranging information in the fields of natural history, archaeology and local history. The Somerset Record Society has been printing English editions of original records of the county's history since 1887, and *Somerset and Dorset Notes and Queries* began to appear shortly afterwards. The contents of these publications must form the basis of any serious study of the county and its parishes.

Modern works on the county, as a whole or in part, include the volumes of the *Victoria County History* for Somerset (four volumes 1906-74, continuing); N. B. Pevsner, *South and West Somerset*, and *North Somerset and Bristol* (Penguin Books 1958); T. J. Hunt and R. R. Sellman, *Aspects of Somerset History* (Somerset County Council 1973); *Christianity in Somerset*, ed. R. W. Dunning (Somerset County Council 1976); R. W. Dunning, *A History of Somerset* (Somerset County Library 1978); and R. W. Dunning, *Somerset and Avon* (Bartholomew 1980). Regional studies within the county include R. Atthill, *Old Mendip* (David and Charles 1971); *Mendip, A New Study*, ed. R. Atthill (David and Charles 1976); and M. Williams, *The Draining of the Somerset Levels* (Cambridge University Press 1970). The latest contribution to the county's natural history is R. G. B. Roe, *The Flora of Somerset* (Somerset Archaeological Society 1981).

Somerset before the Normans

The Archaeology of Somerset, ed. M. Aston and I. Burrow (Somerset County Council 1982) contains the latest statement on archaeological work within the county, with a comprehensive bibliography. The County Museum at Taunton castle, the Roman Baths Museum at Bath, and other museums within the region, contain, of course, most of the artefacts which generations of archaeologists and others have unearthed. Written sources for the Saxon period include *The Anglo-Saxon Chronicle*, ed. D. Whitelock, D. C. Douglas and S. I. Tucker (1965); *English*

Historical Documents I, ed. D. Whitelock (Eyre Methuen 1979); *Memorials of St Dunstan*, ed. W. Stubbs (Rolls Series 1874). H. P. R. Finberg, *Early Charters of Wessex* (Leicester University Press 1964) and G. B. Grundy, *Saxon Charters and field names of Somerset* (Somerset Archaeological Society 1935) are invaluable. R. F. Treharne, *The Glastonbury Legends* (Sphere Books 1971) should be required reading; John Morris, *The Age of Arthur* (Phillimore 1977, 3 vols.) is the wide view of an individualist.

Medieval Somerset

Domesday Book Somerset, ed. C. and F. Thorn (Phillimore 1980) is the latest version of an essential source for both late Saxon England and the early medieval period. Less well used, but equally rewarding, are the published records of central government from the 12th century onwards: Pipe Rolls issued by the Pipe Roll Society from 1884; Patent, Close, Fine, Charter and other rolls, inquisitions, feudal records and deeds issued by the Record Commissioners between 1802 and 1856 and by the Public Record Office from 1864. The volumes of the Somerset Record Society (S.R.S.) include English versions of the cartularies and other records of Athelney, Glastonbury and Muchelney abbeys and Bath, Bruton, Buckland, Montacute and Stogursey priories, and of the estates of the Beauchamps, the Hylles, the Luttrells and the bishops of Winchester. The Historical Manuscripts Commission issued a *Calendar of Wells Cathedral Manuscripts* (2 vols., 1907, 1914). With the volumes of Somerset Feet of Fines and the returns for the 1327 subsidy printed in Kirby's Quest (both S.R.S.), it is possible to trace something of the ownership of most substantial estates in the county and to learn a good deal about their exploitation.

Arms of Hugo Lutterell

All surviving bishops' registers have been reprinted for the county up to the year 1559 in the S.R.S. series, together with a volume of early churchwardens' accounts and two with material on Wells Cathedral (volumes 39 and 56). The first volume also has records of Glastonbury and Bishop Ralph of Shrewsbury's household. The medieval towns of Bath, Bridgwater and Wells have accounts, deeds and charters printed by the S.R.S., adding to the deeds and charters of Bath edited by C. W. Shickle for the Bath Records Society in 1921. The fine series of medieval wills is in four volumes and begins in 1383.

Early Modern Somerset

The Letters and Papers of Henry VIII (1864-1932) and the Patent Rolls from 1547 to the middle of Elizabeth's reign (both printed for the Public Record Office) are essential sources for land ownership changes in the wake of the Dissolution of the monasteries, to be supplemented by two volumes on chantries and their estates in the S.R.S. series. Later ownership of land may be traced in the same series in volumes of Enrolled Deeds and of records of Sales of Wards 1603-41. *The Certificate of Musters, 1569* (S.R.S. 20) gives a list of villagers throughout the county assessed to contribute to the defence of the realm. *Somerset Protestation Returns and Subsidy Rolls*, ed. A. J. Howard and T. L. Stoate (1975) provides lists of the male population in the county in 1641/2. The workings of local government can be found in the records of the Quarter Sessions 1607-76 and in Assize Orders for the county 1629-59 (S.R.S.). These and documents of the Laudian period (S.R.S. 43) have many clues about the coming of Civil War, and some of the fighting itself is described in Sir Ralph Hopton's own account of the 1642-4 campaign (S.R.S. 18). Some of the consequences may be traced in the records of Quakers 1668-99 (S.R.S. 75) and the minutes of the Wells Chapter 1666-83 (S.R.S. 72). Two pioneer works should be consulted: T. G. Barnes, *Somerset, 1625-40* (Oxford University Press 1961) and D. Underdown, *Somerset in the Civil War and Interregnum* (David and Charles 1973). Two other specialist studies have a vast amount of local material on church and social questions which is not apparent from their inadequate indices: G. R. Quaife, *Wanton Wenches and Wayward Wives* (Croom Helm 1979) and M. Stieg, *Laud's Laboratory* (Bucknell University Press, 1982).

The Monmouth Rebellion has inspired many books, the latest and best of which are P. Earle, *Monmouth's Rebels* (1977) and W. M. Wigfield, *The Monmouth Rebellion* (Moonraker 1980).

Modern Somerset

The Somerset Record Society has at yet published no source after 1700 with the exception of two valuable maps of the county, of 1782 and 1822 (S.R.S. 76). Among national records of value for local studies is the series of Parliamentary Papers (Blue Books) which begins in 1715 and includes local material on agriculture, charities, religion, crime and punishment, schools, health, poor relief, employment, censuses and transport. Local newspapers are still largely untapped as a source; they are listed by L. E. J. Brooke, *Somerset Newspapers 1725-1960*. From the late 18th century Directories are of increasing value, their historical sections not always reliable, but their contemporary information often not to be found elsewhere.

The parochial and estate holdings of the County Record Office covering the last three centuries become of great value in the absence of printed sources, and local studies will rely heavily on Land Tax Duplicates, Tithe Maps and Deposited Plans for turnpike roads, canals and railways. Drawings, photographs and the once-despised postcard view are all important means of reconstructing a vision of the past. There remain, inevitably, sources still in private custody—property deeds, family accounts, diaries and letters, and above all private memories of the past, their value increasingly recognised by those who realise that even the 20th century is nearly gone.

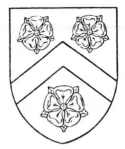

Arms of
Nicholas Wadham

Index

Abbot's Leigh, 69
Abydon, Henry, 51
Acland, Major John Dyke, 80
Adam, Robert, 82
Aethelheard, king, 22
Aethelnoth, ealdorman, 23
Alfoxton, 80
Alfred, king, 23-4, 26; Jewel, 23
Alfred the butler, 27
Alhampton, 87
Allen, Ralph, 77-8, 82; Mr., 100
Aller, 23
Ambrosius Aurelianus, 19
America, 61-3, 80, 89-90, 97
Ancketyll, Henry, 69
Anderdon, Mr., 88
Arch, Joseph, 91
Argyll, earl of, 72
Arthur, 'king', 19-20, 30, 52
Arthur, prince, 31
Arthur, John, monk, 54
Arundel, earl of, 47
Ash Priors, 52
Ashbrittle, 27
Ashcott, *Pipers* inn, 85
Ashe, John, 66
Ashley, Hugh, 76
Ashley Cooper, Anthony, earl of
    Shaftesbury, 71
Ashton, Long, 58; Ashton Court, 60
Ashwick Grove, 87
Asser, bishop, 23
Athelm, bishop, 24
Athelney, 23-4, 90, 101; abbey, 23
Athelstan, king, 24
Attwood, Thomas, 82
Audley, James, 30
Austin, family, 89
Avalon, Hugh of, *see* St Hugh
Avalon, Isle of, 19
Avon, county, 104-5
Axbridge, 24, 27, 36, 43, 45-6, 75, 84

Badon, Mount, 19
Baker, Revd. S. O., 97
Balch, family, 78
Baldwin, Thomas, 82
Baltonsborough, 24, 89
Banwell, 30, 42
Barbay, Abbé, 80
Barrington, 35, 71, 100, 102; Barring-
    ton Court, 61, 85
Bason Bridge, 95
Bath, Adelard of, 51
Bath (Acemannesceaster), 18-22, 24,
    26, 29, 31, 43-7, 68, 74, 77-8, 82,
    84-5, 90, 93, 97, 104; abbey/

Bath (*continued*)
    cathedral priory, 26, 40, 45-6, 82;
    baths, 29, 31, 82; Guildhall, 45;
    St Mary Stalls, 45; St Michael's,
    52; Trinity, 52; *White Hart* inn, 86
Bath, bishops of, 34, 49, 51, 107
Bath and Glastonbury, bishops of,
    49, 107
Bath and Wells, bishops of, 38, 45,
    49, 88, 107-8; diocese of, 33
Bathpool, 46
Bawdrip, 36
Beauchamp, Lady Cecily, 36
Beaufiz, Thomas, 30
Beaufort, duke of, 74
Beckery island, 21
Beckford, Alderman, 84
Beckington, Thomas, bishop, 49, 51
Beckington, 40, 66
Beedall, Thomas, 77
Beercrocombe, 89
Bere, Richard, abbot, 24, 54
Berkeley, Charles, 66; family, 65
Berkley, 78
Bernard, James, 88
Best, Richard, 45
Biddesham, 33
Billingsley, John, 87-8
Binegar, 40
Bishop, Henry, 46
Bishops Hull, 54
Bishops Lydeard, 42, 54, 84, 102
Blackford, 42
Blackmoor (in Cannington), 41, 58
Blake, Benjamin, 63; Joseph, 63;
    Robert, 63, 65, 68
Bleadon, 35-6
Blois, Henry of, abbot, 29
Bluet, Sir Ralph, 30; family, 54
Blund, Stephen le, 32
Bolesdun, Humphrey de, 30
Bonville, William, Lord Bonville, 31;
    Sir William, 33; family, 57
Bovet, Richard, 72
Bradford family, 91, 102
Bradford, 52
Bradley Hill, 18
Brean Down, 18
Brentmarsh, 33
Bretell, Richard, 33
Bridgwater, 29-30, 32-3, 36, 39, 43-4,
    46-7, 52, 58, 61-2, 65-6, 68-9, 71-2,
    74-5, 78, 82, 84, 87, 89, 93, 95, 97,
    99; castle, 29, 44; friary, 47, 50;
    Haygrove, 47; inn, 85; St John's
    Hospital, 30, 47
Brindley, James, 93

122

Brislington, 18
Bristol, 29, 36, 39, 47, 52, 61, 68,
    72, 74, 82, 84-5, 93, 97, 103-4;
    Channel, 11, 24, 93, 99; friars at,
    40; Redcliffe, 44
Broadway, 31
Brompton Ralph, 62
Brooke, Sir Thomas, 33; family, 57, 60
Brown, Lancelot (Capability), 77
Brunel, I. K., 95
Brushford, 34
Bruton, Canon Richard, 30
Bruton, 26-7, 40, 43, 45-7, 95, 99;
    priory/abbey, 50
Brymore, 65
Brympton D'Evercy, 35, 60, 71
Bubwith, Nicholas, bishop, 49, 51
Buckland, priory, 58
Buckland, West, 42
Burnell, Robert, bishop, 30
Burnham, 24, 95, 103
Burrington, 15; Burrington Combe, 97
Burrow Mump, 101
Burton Pynsent, 77, 84-5, 87
Butcombe, 18
Butleigh, 80
Button, William, bishop, 51

Cadbury, North, 54, 61
Cadbury, South, 16-19, 26
Cadbury Congresbury, 19
Camel, West, 88
Cameley, 55
Camerton, 18, 87, 93
Cannington, 20, 24, 41, 58, 90, 105;
    nunnery, 50, 58; and see Blackmoor,
    Brymore
Capton, 36
Carent, family, 54
Carhampton, 22, 24, 39
Carter, John, 52
Castle Cary, 29, 69, 84-5, 89, 95
Caswell, Clement, 69
Catsgore, 18
Cavell, Thomas, 62
Ceawlin, 21
Cenred, 22
Cenwealh, king, 21
Chapman, John, 40
Chard, Thomas, prior, 50
Chard, 42, 45, 66, 71-2, 82, 84, 87,
    89, 102; canal, 95
Charlinch, 62
Charterhouse on Mendip, 18, 41
Chaundler, Thomas, 51
Cheddar, 15, 24, 27, 42, 87, 97, 105
Chedzoy, 71, 75
Chew Magna, 29
Chew Stoke, 54
Chewton Mendip, 41, 68
Chipstable, 54, 89, 101
Chokke, Sir Richard, 57

Churchill, John, Lord Churchill, 72, 74
Churchill, 103
Clark, family, 102
Claverton, 42
Cleaves, George, 62
Cleeve, abbey, 50-1; Our Lady of, 52
Clement, 47
Clevedon, 30, 95, 99
Cnut, king, 26
Coker, East, 32, 62
Cole, Agnes, 52
Cole, 95
Coleridge, William, 80
Coles, Revd. J. S., 91
Combe Hay, 93
Combwich, 18
Compton, John, 40
Compton Bishop, 42, 45
Compton Dundon, 101
Compton Durville, 91
Compton Martin, 51
Congresbury, 27; fair, 97; and see
    Cadbury Congresbury
Cooper, William 80
Corewyll, William, 33-4
Corston, 87
Coryate, Thomas, 62
Cothelstone, 69
Courceulles, Roger de, 27
Courtenay, Sir Peter, 32-3
Crabhole, 44
Crandon Bridge, 18
Creechbarrow (Cructan, Crycbeorh), 21
Crewkerne, 24, 26, 31, 35, 43, 45, 58,
    68-9, 82, 84-5, 95, 105; and see
    Woolminstone
Cricket St Thomas, 80, 85
Croscombe, 52
Crosse, Robert, 62
Crowcombe, 88
Culbone, 52
Curry, North, 36-7, 45; Newport, 45
Curry Mallet, 29, 80
Curry Rivel, 13, 77
Cuthwine, 21
Cynegils, king, 21
Cynewulf, king, 22

Dare, Thomas, 71-2
Darlington, Lord, 79
Daubeney, Giles, Lord Daubeney, 47,
    57; Henry, Lord Daubeney, earl of
    Bridgwater, 57, 61
Davis, family, 38
Day, Mr., 87
Dening, family, 102
Devon, earl of, 31
Dillington, 77
Dinnington, 41
Disraeli, Benjamin, 79
Dodge, Nicholas, 62

Dodington, Sir Francis, 66; George (Bubb), 78; family, 78
Dolyng, Watkyn, 33
Doulting, 21, 41
Dowai, Walter de, 27
Dowlish Wake, 81
Downend, 45
Drake, Sir Francis, 62
Droxford, John, bishop, 30
Dulverton, 27, 34, 88
Dummer, Captain, 75
Dundry, 41, 52, 65, 84
Dunkerton, 93
Dunster, 29, 32-3, 36, 52, 61, 66, 68-9, 88; castle, 50

Eadnoth the Staller, 27
Eadred, king, 24
Eadwig, king, 24
Eanwulf, ealdorman, 22
Easton in Gordano, 52
Edgar, king, 24
Edingworth, 18
Edith, 27
Edmund, king, 24
Edmund Ironside, king, 26
Egbert, king, 22
Egremont, Lord, 89
Elliot, family, 62
Elworthy, 69, 89
Engilby, Thomas, 30
Enmore, 32, 44, 78
Essex, earl of, 58, 68
Ethelred I, 22-3
Ethelred II, 26
Evercreech, 95
Exmoor forest, 41
Exton, 101

Falaise, William de, 27, 50
Farleigh Hungerford, 32, 57, 68
Farnaby, Thomas, 99 ·
Fawkes, Guy, 58, 60
Feversham, Lord, 74
Fiennes, Celia, 82
Fivehead, 13
Fox, family, 102
Foxcote, 87
Frobisher, Sir Martin, 62
Frome, John, 33-4
From, 21, 24, 27, 43, 46-7, 74, 79, 82, 84, 89, 93, 95, 97
Frye, John, 66
Fussell, Mr., 93

Galmington, 101; tithing, 36
Gapper, Mr., 85
Gascoigne, Thomas, 51
Gateryn, Thomas, 41
Gaunt, John of, 32
Geraint, king, 22
Gese, Thomas, 33

Glasier, John, 52
Glastonbury, 17-19, 29-30, 40-1, 45-6, 72, 74-5, 84, 86, 88, 95, 97; abbey, 19, 21-2, 24, 26, 29-30, 38, 42, 44, 46, 51-2, 54, 58; abbots, 39, 50, 58; St John's church, 52, 54; Tor, 19, 54
Glendower, Owen, 30, 32
Godney, 21
Godwine, Earl, 26
Gorges, Sir Ferdinando, 62; family, 58
Gorsey Bigbury, 16
Gothelney, 57
Gould, John, 88
Gournay, Sir Matthew, 32
Gouvis, Brian de, 30
Green, James, 95
Greenham, 95
Gregory, Thomas, 62
Grey, Lord, 72
Grove, Henry, 99
Gryme, John, 52
Guinevere, 'queen', 19, 30, 52
Gunthorpe, John, dean, 31
Gurdun, Adam, 29
Guthrum, 23

Hadley, James, 52
Halliday, William, 100
Halse, 52, 88
Halswell, 78
Ham, 91
Ham, Low, 69-70, 97
Ham, High, 99
Hammet, Sir Benjamin, 78
Harewell, John, bishop, 49
Harold, Earl, king, 26-7
Harptree, East, 29, 41, 99; castle, 29
Harrys, John, 52
Haselbury Plucknett, 51
Hastings, family, 54
Hatch Beauchamp, 27, 36
Henlade, 88
Heremann the German, 34
Hervey, Revd. Sydenham, 91
Highbridge, 90, 97; wharf, 95
Hill, William, 60
Hinton Blewett, 30
Hinton Charterhouse, priory, 40, 50
Hinton St George, 58, 60, 69, 71, 78
Hirrin, John, 75
Hoare, Henry, 84
Hobhouse, Rt. Hon. Henry, 103
Hody, John, 99; family, 57
Holbrook, Mr., 87
Holes, Andrew, 51
Holland, Parson, 81-2
Hood, Alexander, Viscount Bridport, 80; Samuel, Viscount Hood, 80; Revd. Samuel, 80; family, 80, 102
Hopton, Sir Ralph, 58, 65-6
Horner, Jack, 58; Sir John, 66; family, 58, 102

Horrington, 55
Houndstreet, Marksbury, 58
Howell, Samuel, 89
Huish, Alexander, 66
Huish Episcopi, 41-2
Hull(e), Sir Edward, 32-3; Robert, 54
Hungerford, Sir Walter, 32
Hutchins, Thomas, 82
Huntworth, 47, 58, 93
Huppehull, Gilbert, 36
Hurley, Richard, 88
Hutton, 103
Hygons, Richard, 51

Ilchester (Lindinis), 18, 26, 29-30, 35-
    6, 43-4, 46-7, 50, 78-9, 84, 88
Ilminster, 31, 45, 65, 89-90, 99-100
Ine, king, 21-2
Isle Brewers, 71

Jeanes, Mr., 87
Jefferies, family, 52
Jeffreys, Lord Chief Justice, 75
John the Old Saxon, 23
Jones, Inigo, 61
Joyce, William, 49

Ken, Thomas, bishop, 76
Kendall, John, 44
Kent, Walter de, 30
Kentsford, 69
Kerry, John, 62
Keynsham, 22, 27, 74; abbey, 50
Kilmersdon, 54, 88
Kilton, 24, 39
Kilvert, Francis, 97
Kingsbury Episcopi, 42
Kingsdon, 30
Kirk, Colonel, 75
Kirton, Edward, 69
Knight, John, 88
Knowle St Giles, 62

Lamyatt, 18
Langport, 23, 36, 43-7, 68, 77, 84-5,
    95, 97
Langton, John de, 30
Lansdown, battle, 68
Laud, William, archbishop, 65
Launcherley, 49
Leach, James, 62
Leigh on Mendip, 58
Lewes, Robert of, bishop, 29, 43, 49
Lilstock, 93, 99
Litson, Alexander, 80
Littleton, 18
Lock, Adam, 49
Lockyer, Thomas, 78; family, 78
Lopen, 60
Lovel, Ralph, 29
Lovington, 85
Lower Weare, 45

Lowman, Mr., 87
Lucca, Fortunatus de, 29
Lufton, 58
Luttrell, Sir Hugh, 32; J. F., 88; Sir
    James, 57; Sir John, 61; Temple, 79;
    Lady, 61; family, 39, 57, 78, 102
Lydeard St Lawrence, 80
Lygh, Thomas, 55
Lyng, 24
Lyte, Henry, 61
Lytes Cary, 61

Macadam, J. L., 85
Malory, Sir Thomas, 19
Manners, Sir William, 78-9, 84
March, William of, bishop, 30
Marchey, 21
Mare, John de la, 32
Mareys, John, 52
Mark, 87, 103
Marksbury, 58
Marshall's Elm, 66
Marshwood, 61
Marston Magna, 36
Martock, 30, 95, 99
Maundown, Wiveliscombe, 101
Maurice, Prince, 68
Meare, 17, 21, 41
Medlycott, Thomas Hutchings, 79
Mells, 58, 69, 93
Melwas, King of Somerset, 19
Mendip forest, 41
Merrifield, 36
Merriott, 42, 97
Middleney, Sir Ralph of, 32
Middlezoy, 89
Midford, 93
Milborne Port, 43, 46, 78-9
Milverton, 43, 54, 72
Minehead, 47, 61-2, 78-9, 84, 95, 99
Mitchell, George, 90-1
Mohun, William de, 27, 29; family, 50
Monmouth, Geoffrey of, 19
Montacute, William de, earl of Salisbury,
    32
Montacute, 18, 27, 29, 45, 58, 60, 65,
    78, 90; Montacute House, 60-1;
    priory, 45, 50-1, 60
Montagud, Drew de, 27
Montfort, Peter de, 29-30, Simon de, 29
Mora, William de, 36
More, Hannah, 100
Morgan, Mr., 87
Morris, Dr. Claver, 85
Mortain, count of, 27, 30
Morton, John, archbishop, 31
Moxham, William, 88
Muchelney, 97; abbey, 21-2, 41, 50
Mullett, A. A., 89

Nailsea Court, 61
Nash, Richard (Beau), 77, 82

Nelson, Horatio, 82
Neroche forest, 41
Nether Stowey, 76, 80, 85
Nethway, William, 45
Nettlebridge, 93
Nettlecombe, 32, 58, 61-2, 78
Neville, Richard (Kingmaker), earl of
    Warwick, 31; family, 44
Newton, Sir John, 58; Revd. William, 80
Newton Surmaville, 61
North, Frederick, Lord North, earl of
    Guilford, 77-9
Norton, Robert, 52
Norton Fitzwarren, 17, 95
Norton St Philip, 40, 52, 74
Nunney, 32, 58; castle, 32
Nyland, 21
Nynehead, 30

Odcombe, 62
Offa, king, 22
Old Cleeve, 27, 80
Oliver, Dr. William, 82
Orchard Portman, 85
Orchard Wyndham, 58, 76-8
Othery, 55, 89
Otterford, 13
Over Stowey, 80

Pagan's Hill, 18
Palmer, Thomas, 60
Parcet, Elizabeth, 71
Parsons, White, 88; Mr., 88
Paschall, Andrew, 71, 75
Pennard, West, 55
Penselwood, battle, 21, 26
Pensford, 74, 84
Perceval, lords Egmont, family, 78
Peren, W. B., 91
Pery, John, 47
Petherton, North, 46; forest, 41
Petherton, South, 43, 57, 91, 103
Phelips, Sir Edward, 60, 62; Edward,
    78; Sir Robert, 60, 65-6, 77; Robert,
    of Salisbury, 69; Thomas, 58, 60
Piers, William, bishop, 65-6, 70; Wil-
    liam, son of, 69
Pill, 103
Pitminster, 62; *and see* Poundisford
Pitney, 18
Pitt, William, earl of Chatham, 77, 84,
    87, 91
Pixton, 80
Plantagenet, Edward, earl of Warwick,
    57; George, duke of Clarence, 31,
    57; Margaret, 57
Plummer, Christopher, 31
Poole, Tom, 80
Popham, Alexander, 58; Edward, 66;
    Sir John, 58; family, 58
Porlock, 24, 26, 99
Portishead, 13

Portman, Sir William, 66, 76, 85
Poster, Mr., 87
Poulett, Sir Amias (d. 1538), 58, 60-1;
    Sir Amias (d. 1588), 60; Sir Hugh,
    60-1; John, 1st baron, 60, 66, 69;
    John, 2nd baron, 71; John, 4th earl,
    81; family, 58, 60-1, 78
Poundisford, Lodge, 61; Park, 60
Preston, Amias, 62
Priddy, 36, 40-1; stone circle, 16
Prowse, Thomas, 78
Prynne, William, 65
Puriton, 104
Pym, John, 65-6, 77
Pyne, John, 66
Pynsent, Sir William, 77

Quantoxhead, East, 61; West, 85
Queen Camel, 30

Rackley, 45
Raddington, 38, 101
Radstock, 93, 95
Ralegh, John de, 32; Simon de, 32;
    family, 58
Raleigh, Sir Walter, 58, 60; Walter,
    dean of Wells, 69
Reginald, bishop, 49
Rennie, John, 93
Rimpton, 36, 42
Robert the Constable, 27
Rodney, Sir Edward, 66; George,
    Baron Rodney, 80; family, 58
Rodney Stoke, 80
Rogers, Sir Edward, 58; Squire, 88
Rooksmill, 44

St Aldhelm, 21-2, 26
St Alfheah, bishop, 26
St·Catherine, 61
St Clair, Bretel de, 27
St Dunstan, 24, 26
St Hugh of Lincoln, 50
Salisbury, earls of, 57
Sampford Brett, 88
Sandford, 103
Scott, James, duke of Monmouth, 63,
    71-6, 84
Seavington, 41
Sedgemoor, 71; battle of, 63, 80;
    King's, 88; West, 87, 104
Selleck, John, 69
Selwood, forest, 41
Semson, Roger, 52
Seymour, William, marquess of Hert-
    ford, 66
Shapwick, 103
Shepton Beauchamp, 35, 89, 91, 102
Shepton Mallet, 18, 36, 47, 54, 72,
    74, 84, 87, 95, 99
Shepton Montague, 27
Shetler, Charles, 101

126

Shrewsbury, Ralph of, bishop, 30, 42, 46
Simon the Armurer, 34
Simonsbath, 88
Siward the Hawker, 41
Smith, John, the Fleming, 47; Revd. Sydney, 79; Mr. 87
Smyth, John, 39-40; family, 61
Sock Dennis, 29
Solsbury, Little, 19
Somer, Thomas, 34
Somerset Co. Council, 97, 101-3, 105
Somerset, duke of, 74; earl of, 34
Somerton, 18, 22-4, 27, 30, 45-6, 74, 81, 84-5; *and see* Bradley Hill, Catsgore
Southwick, 45
Spaxton, 54
Speke, Anne (wife of Lord North) 77; George, 71-2; Mr. 87, 91
Stafford, Humphrey, earl of Devon, 44
Stanton Drew, 16
Stavordale, priory, 50
Stawell, George, 69-70; Sir John, 69; Ralph, 70
Stayner, Gilbert, 52
Steepholm, 24
Sterne, Richard, 69
Stoford, 45
Stogumber, 62; Rowden, 35
Stogursey, 17, 41, 50, 52, 76; Fairfield, 60; priory, 50
Stoke sub Hamdon, 35-6, 91; castle, 32
Stoney Littleton, 16
Stourton, family, 57
Stratton on the Fosse, 41
Street, 66, 102
Strode, William, 66, 71
Surland, Richard, 31
Sutton, Long, 68
Sutton Wick, 58
Swainswick, 65
Swein, earl, 26; Forkbeard, 26
Sydenham, Sir George, 62; John, 30; John (another), 71; family, 58, 61
Sydenham, 30

Talbot, Geoffrey, 29
Tanner, Thomas, 44
Taunton, John, abbot, 30
Taunton, 21, 29, 31, 33, 43-4, 46-7, 61-2, 65-6, 68-9, 71-2, 75, 78, 84, 89, 93, 95, 97, 99, 102-4; castle, 29, 31, 36, 41; castle hall, 79; *Castle* inn, 85; Galmington tithing, 36; Holway tithing, 36; minster, 22; priory, 50; St Mary's church, 45; St Saviour, 52; *and see* Wilton
Templecombe, 95
Timsbury, 93
Tofig, sheriff, 27
Toms, John, 89

Tose, John, 46
Tratt, Driver, 102
Treat, Richard, 62
Tremaille, Thomas, 41, 58
Trent, 69
Trevelyan, John (15th cent.) '58; Sir John (16th cent.), 61; Sir John (18th cent.), 78; William, 62
Trull, 97
Tucker, Richard, 52
Tudway, family, 78
Tuse, Alexander, 46
Twerton, 26, 87
Tynte, Charles Kemeys, 78

Ven, 78
Villula, John de, bishop, 51
Virgin, Anne, daughter of, 85
Vox, Walter, 36

Wade, George, 78; Nathaniel, 72
Wadeford, 18
Wadham, family, 58
Wakelyn, John, 54
Waleys, Nicholas, 46
Walsingham, Sir Francis, 60
Walter, Edward, 78-9
Walton Heath, 16
Walwyn, Mr., 88
Warwick, earls of, 57
Watchet, 24, 26, 36, 43, 95, 99; Cleeve Hill, 43; St Decuman's church, 43, 69, 76
Wedmore, 24, 27, 88; Peace of, 23-4
Wellington, 38-9, 42, 58, 72, 102; St Laurence's chapel, 39
Wellisford, 95
Wellow, 18, 93
Wells, Hugh of, 29; Jocelin of (Jocelin Trotman), bishop, 45, 49
Wells, 16, 26, 29-31, 33, 36, 43-4, 46-7, 49, 51-2, 55, 66, 69, 71, 74-5, 78, 80, 84-5, 95, 97, 99; bishops of, 49, 51; cathedral, 49, 51, 86; chapter, 45; minster, 22; Palace, 30-1, 46; St Cuthbert's church, 44, 55; *Swan* inn, 86
Wembdon, 52
Wemberham, 18
Westhay, 16
Weston super Mare, 95, 97, 99, 103
Weston Zoyland, 74-5, 88-9
Wheeler, James, 66
White, family, 102
Whitelackington, 71
Whiting, Richard, abbot, 24, 54
Wiars, Thomas, 62
Widow, Robert, 51
Wilfred, Roger, monk, 54
Willcox, S. L., 90
Williams, John, 30
Williton, 69, 99; hundred, 88

127

Wilton, 102
Wiltshire, earl of, 31
Wimbridge, John, 80
Wincanton, 82, 84
Winford, 52, 54
Winsford Hill, 20; Caratacus stone, 20
Witham, John, 61
Witham, priory, 40, 50, 58
Withycombe, 52, 88, 103
Wiveliscombe, 18, 38, 42, 88-9, 101
Wolsey, Thomas, cardinal, 58
Wood, John, father and son, 77, 82
Wookey, 30
Woolavington, 57, 99
Woolminstone, 13
Woolverton, 87
Wordsworth, Dorothy, 80; William, 80
Wotton, George, 69
Wraxall, 62, 69

Writhlington, 93
Wulfric of Haselbury, 51
Wylle, Robert, 36
Wylly, Roger, 33
Wyndham, Edmund, 66; Francis, 68-9;
    Sir Hugh, 69; John, 58; Thomas,
    61-2; Sir William, 77-8; family, 78
Wynford, William, 49, 52

Yarlington, 88
Yatton, 42, 52, 54, 97
Yeovil, 31, 35, 43, 47, 52, 82, 87, 95,
    97, 102; St John's church, 45
Yeovilton, 69, 105
Yerbery, John, 40
York, Richard, duke of, 31
Yorke, Mr., 38
Yonge, John, 51
Young, Mr., 87